D1375164

PEAKS
AND
BANDITS

THE CLASSIC OF
NORWEGIAN LITERATURE

PEAKS AND BANDITS

ALF BONNEVIE BRYN

TRANSLATED BY BIBBI LEE

Vertebrate Publishing, Sheffield
www.v-publishing.co.uk

THE CLASSIC OF
NORWEGIAN LITERATURE

PEAKS
AND
BANDITS

Alf Bonnevie Bryn

First published in Norway by Johan Grundt Tanum under the title
Tinder og Banditter in 1943.
Republished in 2012 by Vagabond Forlag/Travellers Press, Norway.
This edition first published in 2021 by Vertebrate Publishing.

 Vertebrate Publishing
Omega Court, 352 Cemetery Road, Sheffield, S11 8FT, United Kingdom
www.v-publishing.co.uk

NORLA
Norwegian
Literature Abroad

This translation has been published with the financial support of NORLA.

Copyright © Vagabond Forlag AS, 2003.
Translation copyright © Bibbi Lee, 2016.
Cover illustration © Editions Nevicata/Aline Baudet.

Vagabond Forlag AS have asserted their rights under the Copyright, Designs and Patents
Act 1988 to be identified as the rights holder of this work.

This book is a work of non-fiction based on the life, experiences and recollections of Alf
Bonnevie Bryn. In some limited cases the names of people, places, dates and sequences
or the detail of events have been changed solely to protect the privacy of others.

A CIP catalogue record for this book is available from the British Library.

ISBN 978-1-83981-048-0 (Hardback)
ISBN 978-1-83981-086-2 (Paperback)
ISBN 978-1-83981-054-1 (Ebook)

10 9 8 7 6 5 4 3 2 1

All rights reserved. No part of this work covered by the copyright herein
may be reproduced or used in any form or by any means – graphic, electronic,
or mechanised, including photocopying, recording, taping or information storage
and retrieval systems – without the written permission of the publisher.

Every effort has been made to obtain the necessary permissions with reference to
copyright material, both illustrative and quoted. We apologise for any omissions in
this respect and will be pleased to make the appropriate acknowledgements in any
future edition.

Cover design by Jane Beagley, production by Cameron Bonser,
Vertebrate Publishing. www.v-publishing.co.uk

Vertebrate Publishing is committed to printing on paper from sustainable sources.

 **MIX**
Paper from
responsible sources
FSC® C018072

Printed and bound in Great Britain by Clays Ltd, Elcograf S.p.A.

Contents

Prelude in Switzerland

Quite late one Sunday evening in August 1909, I was hanging from a rope down the south side of Gross Ruchen.

I was hanging with my head down some eighteen to twenty-one feet under the top ridge. On the other side of the ridge, about the same distance down the north slope, hung Max van Heyden van der Slaat. Straddling the ridge right behind us sat George Ingle Finch, who was tied to the same rope. He had a big, heavy backpack with self-recording meteorological instruments on his back.

The immediate cause of finding myself in this annoying position was that a piece of the ridge, astride which Max had been edging forward, had broken off and sailed down – along with Max. To prevent all three of us from going the same way, I had slid down the south side and flipped around as the rope tightened. This, incidentally, is an example of the regular procedure in this kind of situation. I knew this from the literature, but it was the first time I had personally used the technique.

It seemed quite frightening. The first time at any rate. A feeling somewhat like letting oneself go off a high ski jump, or diving into cold water from a great height. It's just that, as a rule, one has more of an opportunity to get used to those things. Parachuting out of airplanes was not in vogue then, or else that would have been the closest comparison.

It has been said that in those apparently life-threatening moments, your whole life passes before you in the blink of an eye. Childhood memories and your home appear, and you regret things you have done or failed to do. This does not tally with my experiences. The only thing I can remember thinking of as I rushed down the wall of ice was whether Max was solidly tied to the rope. Not that I was particularly worried about his fate, but he did have the vitally important task of being the counterweight and obstacle to my continuing journey. Thank God Max was sitting firmly and the rope held.

Considerably worse, or much more exciting anyway, was the case of O.G. Jones who climbed Dent Blanche in 1887 with his friend (or so he thought) Dr H. Robinson. They had left Zermatt the day before to ascend Dent Blanche by a particularly difficult route, which for some reason had acquired the name Arête des Quatre Ânes (The Four Donkeys Ridge). As you approach the summit of Dent Blanche, the landscape looks about the same as the ridge toward the top of Gross Ruchen, the only difference being that the elevation is considerably higher and the north face practically sheer for the first 900 to 1,200 feet. Then it gradually becomes a slick ice wall, which after a while slopes off and ends in a glacier about 4,500 feet below the summit. The drop on the south side is almost equally high but not quite so steep.

A mean wind was blowing with quite a bit of snowdrift, and Jones could barely see Robinson, who was walking about forty-five feet ahead of him on the rope. He saw Robinson lose his footing and begin to slide, after which he turned himself outward and disappeared. This was due to Robinson having untied himself from the rope before he slid, so that Jones took all the rope with him on the rest of his journey down. Robinson managed to stop his slide with the help of his ice axe and remained on the top of the ridge.

What Jones did not know was that his friend had just discovered that he had been having a relationship with Mrs Robinson for some time – something that in the bigoted, bourgeois English circles of the day was regarded as being against good form.

Robinson had a tough time getting back down from the top of Dent Blanche. He had to spend two nights in the open and arrived in Zermatt extremely bedraggled, but pleased to have saved the family honour in such a clever way.

In a cafe in Zermatt he found his friend Jones and Mrs Robinson fortifying themselves with a cup of tea after having spent a success-ful night in a hotel. It turned out that Jones had made it, without a scratch, from the top ridge of Dent Blanche down to the glacier 4,500 feet below, with the help of a big avalanche. He had been a little confused but had regained consciousness on the glacier, and then spent the night in a cabin not far away before walking down to Zermatt. After organising the rescue operation for his friend left behind, he could in good conscience turn his attention to what he took to be the widow.

This story is recorded (minus some of the details and explanations I have provided) in the *Alpine Journal* of 1888. Though there is nothing to indicate how family relations developed from then on.

Complications of the Robinson–Jones kind did not exist between Max and me – we were both unmarried. Besides, it wasn't Max who had planned the trip; on the contrary, it was with some reluctance that he had come along on the ascent, his first (and probably also his last).

Max van Heyden van der Slaat was not Dutch, as his name would suggest. In his youth his father had moved to Russia, where he had made a huge fortune and was the owner of one of the country's biggest rubber factories and a number of forest properties, among other things. But Max was no plutocrat's son. He frequented shady characters and became a member of revolutionary student circles. As this corresponded badly with his father's business interests, he sent Max to Zurich to study. He sent him away with an elderly servant and a million francs, meant to last the entire duration of study.

Of all the cities in Europe at that time Zurich was the worst choice for someone meant to be kept away from dawning Bolshevism. It was there that the organisation which would eight years later become the revolution was formed. And it was there that Ulyanov[1] sat in his lodgings or his favourite pub lecturing about Marx, Engels and himself to an ever-larger circle of male and female admirers.

---

1 Vladimir Ulyanov, better known under his *nom de guerre* Lenin.

On the periphery of this circle hovered Max, who very quickly put his studies aside in order to dedicate himself to a niece of the Russian painter Vereshchagin – a relationship that nonetheless gave him more sorrow than joy. So it was her fault that Max was hanging where he was.

The previous history was this: one evening I was at a small and simple variety theatre watching a performance by professional boxers. As far as I can remember, the match was between the Battling Kid, champion of Missouri, and Pete, the Terror of Milwaukee, who were giving a very average demonstration of the noble art. After the act, the director came on stage and announced an award of 100 francs to anyone in the audience who could hold his own for three minutes against one of the professionals.

For a long time this had been a popular additional act, something akin to what circuses do when they invite the public to come and stand on the broad back of a horse which is trained to wiggle a little so that the victim is thrown off, to everyone's amusement. But lately the number of volunteer amateur boxers had dwindled, and you had to be satisfied with hired victims who would let themselves be knocked out in a gentle fashion once per evening.

This time, however, we were luckier. A tall, skinny, light-haired youngster calmly rose from his seat in the first row, stepped across the orchestra pit and presented himself. That was the first time I made George's acquaintance. It was also the first time for the Terror of Milwaukee, and for him it was a sad experience.

The fight didn't last a full minute. When Terror hit the floor for the third time, he refused to get up. Poor Terror didn't stand a chance. George's arms were six inches longer than his and he never reached farther than George's left or right glove. He couldn't even sneak in a clinch, every professional boxer's friend and helper when in need. George humbly received the roaring ovation and asked if the Battling Kid didn't also want to go one round. The Battling Kid didn't want to. But then came the great anticlimax: George wasn't paid. No, the deal was for three minutes, this had lasted only one, so no 100 francs. The public probably missed a lot when the discussion between George and the variety show administrators took place behind closed doors.

The members of the administration must have been strong and numerous, because they won the day. When the whole thing was over, I found George out on the corner with Max, who in a much-dishevelled state was in the process of forcing 100 francs on him as a tribute from an admiring public. George was broad-minded in money matters and let himself be convinced.

It so happened that I joined them at a nearby pub, where we were read *Die Leiden des jungen Werthers* (*The Sorrows of Young Werther*).

Max was not having much fun with his Vereshchagin. She really had nothing against him personally, it was just that she was decidedly communistic, even in the erotic sphere. In 1908 she was already in possession of the Bolshevik ideals that would not receive the official stamp until the early 1920s. (History has shown us that even before that time there were several such rascals in Russia, not least on the female side.) As already mentioned, she would make use of Max, but put the common good before his personal interests. Besides, she said, he was no real proletarian. To put it plainly, he was the worst kind of plutocrat, not even worthy of sitting in the same pub as Ulyanov.

'As if I'm not just as good a proletarian as him,' said Max, 'just because my father is rich. Ulyanov's father is an aristocrat – that's not so good either. And how can I help it if I don't have a brother who's been hanged? I don't even have a brother. That's not my fault.

'It doesn't matter what I do,' Max continued as he started on a fresh drink. 'I thought she would find it a nice trait that I paid for a complete meteorological station to be installed at Altstadt, right by her regular cafe.

'"But no, what do I care about the weather in Zurich?" she said. "Just give me a sports outfit." Of course I did that too, and no sooner did she receive it she went away to a cabin with one of those damned Finns – what did he have to brag about? He had shot a policeman in Helsingfors – probably an accidental shot

5

– and there she lies now. Cheers. Women! Damn – now I'm going home – you're my friends – good night.'

Truly a sad fate, being robbed of one's illusions in one's early twenties.

'Listen,' said George after Max had left, 'I think we have to do something for him.'

I agreed. Max considered us his friend. You never let down a friend.

It took a while to find his meteorological station, which was installed in a glass case in an alley where it obviously did not belong. It was full of expensive instruments with clockworks and rotating cylinders. The ingenious part of George's plan was not that we would steal the station. He was a broad-minded organiser, far ahead of his times.

'We'll pack it up,' he said, 'and then we'll bring Max and the station to the top of Gross Ruchen. It's obviously more interesting to determine the weather in places where no one visits than in the middle of town where you feel the weather yourself.'[2]

I have good reason not to reveal how we managed to steal the station. But around three o'clock, with all the instruments securely packed in an old raincoat, we arrived at Zurich's best hotel, Baur au Lac, where Max lived with his servant. It was obvious that Max had made more of an impression on the night porter than on his faithless Bolshevik girlfriend, otherwise we would never have been allowed entry so late at night.

We dragged him out of bed and explained our plan. Max found it only moderately interesting. It was only after George had convinced him that this activity would not only improve his self-esteem, but also bring his faithless girlfriend to understand that she was consorting with a desperate and lawless man, that Max gave in and agreed to participate in the expedition to Gross Ruchen that day.

---

2 It is interesting to note that George, who later became a professor in London, was a real pioneer in this field. Not until many years later did meteorologists, principally at Professor Bjerknes' initiative, begin systematic work to establish stations on high mountain tops. Now there are many of them, in both Switzerland and Norway, but in all fairness George, Max and I should be recognised as pioneers in this field.

And so we were hanging there. The weather was foul and it was getting dark. It is by no means easy to resolve such a situation: it takes its time. Just managing to squirm around to get your head on top is a work of patience, and then you have to hold the rope with one hand and use the ice axe with the other to get a reasonable foothold. George was straddling the ridge above us, directing the operation. He gave the impression of being pleased.

Finally both Max and I regained the top of the ridge and there we sat, all three of us, straddling it. It was about nine o'clock and it had grown quite dark. The snow whirled up with the wind from the north and made a cloud out across the precipice toward the south. Sometimes we could just barely see the contours of stone slabs up toward the main peak in front of us. Before daylight we could go neither forward nor backward.

What does one do in such a situation? Nothing – there is no danger. You can only wait.

We ate cured meat, smoked a pipe and beat our heels against the ice to keep warm. Every once in a while George sang a song for us. He was no great artist. He knew only one song and sang it loudly and off key.

> I loved a lass and her name was Lill
> But she was seduced by Buffalo Bill
> And then she was kissed by Seladon Hill
> God damn her soul, I love her still.

George was born and raised in southern Australia. The fact that he knew this typically American love poem, and that it was also the only poetry he was familiar with, is good proof of how early on the American temperament started to influence even faraway areas of the globe.

There is little to be said about the rest of our meteorological expedition. I've never heard another thing about those instruments we so carefully built into a cairn at the top the next morning.

About Max van Heyden van der Slaat, there is really nothing to say other than what is said about most men in Norwegian history – he is no longer part of this saga. He was just an incidental part of this prelude, which started my acquaintance with George and which some time later led us to decide to discover Corsica.

Preparations, financing and provisioning

With whom the plan to explore Corsica originated will probably never be determined with any certainty. The available professional literature gives contradictory information. For example, you will find in *The Norwegian Tourist Association Yearbook* a short account of the expedition and its results from which it appears that the initiative came from the Norwegian side. That account was written by me. If, on the other hand, you seek information from the *Alpine Journal*, wherein the journey is also described, you get the distinct impression that the original idea was Australian. The account in the *Alpine Journal* was written by George. A third version, no doubt the most diplomatic, may be found in the work entitled *The Making of a Mountaineer*, wherein George magnanimously lets us each get the idea independently.

Personally I no longer have an opinion about this international question of prestige, but it would not surprise me to find that the original version in the *Alpine Journal* was the right one. I clearly do remember that, according to plans approved by the powers that be on the home front, I was supposed to spend Easter vacation 1909 in Lausanne studying French. What is certain, however, is that George and I, a few weeks before the start of the vacation, had become clear about needing to go to Corsica.

The plan was quickly made, but then there was the question of obtaining permission from the Australian and Norwegian authorities. We discussed this back and forth. It would obviously in many ways have been a considerable relief, financially among other things, if the expedition could begin in a formal, official manner. But on the other hand, should the plans not meet with approval – and we thought there was much to indicate that this might be the case – then the consequences would be considerably more serious than if we started without ever seeking prior approval; almost without prohibition.

The solution we finally reached, all things considered, was certainly the right one. Like all ingenious solutions, it was tremendously simple. At a point so late that no order to desist could reach us, we would both write home and say that we had had to change our previously approved Easter plans because we had been invited by a well-off friend – George by me and me by George – to travel to northern Italy and Corsica.

There were still obstacles in our way, for our ingenious solution required making financial arrangements. The financing of voyages of discovery has always posed difficult problems for the organisers. The idealised values connected to something being discovered, no matter what it is, as a rule have completely escaped the sensibilities of financial matadors. When the explorer cannot bring mercantile interests into his plans, like Columbus and Marco Polo, or be like Henry Morton Stanley, who had a wealthy newspaper behind him, then he faces financial difficulties that often seem insurmountable.

When you think about it, it was worse for us than for our predecessors. They could, at any rate, present their plans officially and appeal to whatever interests might exist. We were excluded from this possibility. There have been great discoverers both before and after George and me – I am too high-minded to want to rob them of the fame they have won – but one must not forget that for them the really big difficulties were solved by others, whereas we had to solve them ourselves.

We created a financial plan. The journey to Corsica via Genoa, Livorno and Bastia, then back to Zurich via Ajaccio and Nice in third class (and fourth where it existed) at that time cost approximately 200 francs. Room and board for six weeks we figured at 250 francs, when we allowed for a total of six nights under a roof. The rest of the time we would sleep outdoors. Adding 50 francs for unforeseen expenses, the total came to 500 francs each. Half of this sum would be covered by the last month's stipend if we didn't pay the rent and other debt. The rest we had to dredge up.

As students abroad you don't have an opportunity to make extra income except by 'buying' expensive books and instruments, which you don't actually acquire but rather borrow from friends. As far as our library was concerned, both George and I at that time had such a hypothetical one that no prospects of any amount of luck worth mentioning could increase it.

'But,' said George after some reflection, 'I have a spirit level!' George was a chemistry student, and as a rule there are no levels in the chemistry department. And the level was not really his; he had confiscated it from a friend in the building department. He knew someone who would pay 300 francs for it. This may sound strange, but anyone who has studied at a technical college will know that we all need a level. You receive money from home to buy it and then sell it right away. In the four years I spent at the college in Zurich, I came across only one level among the Nordic students and conservatively speaking that must have cost gullible Nordic parents an average of 15,000 francs a year.

'There is no reason,' I said, 'that you should sell it to him. Sell it to me, I'll resell it, then that'll make 600 francs.' That's how easy it was to solve these financial problems that looked so difficult before we took them on.

But financing also had other sides. For some reason we had the fixed idea that foreigners travelling through Italy were faced with a high degree of swindle. George in particular had a deep mistrust of the Italians and was determined that we must guard in every possible way against being cheated. Convinced that attack is the best defence, we therefore decided to acquire a reserve of counter-feit money.

Money matters at that time were quite particular. First of all, it so happened that Swiss, French and Italian silver coins were valid in all these countries. But there were also some older Greek coins of the same appearance as the five franc and five lire pieces. These had also been valid at some point but now they were out of circulation. Such Greek coins were freely exchanged for their worth in silver (about two francs) and were continuously in circulation, aided by people with a highly developed sense of saving.

Now we reasoned as follows: there was every reason to believe that we would have worthless coins pressed upon us, particularly since we as foreigners couldn't see the difference at all. It is therefore just as well that we insure ourselves by bringing our own supply of them. On the basis of today's more advanced ideology, this may be understood as a form of anticipated retaliation.

After the financial problems had found a happy solution, we proceeded to the second main problem that all journeys of discovery have in common: the question of equipment.

Here arose at the beginning some differences of opinion related to the fact that Australia at that time was an entirely undiscovered country, believed to be principally inhabited by cannibals. George was of the opinion that this must also be the case in Corsica and that the different chiefs on this relatively unknown island should be pacified with gifts of glass beads, bells, mirrors and the like, which had been the conventional currency of safaris among tribes.

It was very difficult to convince him that this would be unnecessary baggage, and it was really only when I showed him Baedeker's excellent guide to Corsica that he, much against his will, had to reconcile himself to the fact that we were too late to be doing business on the same basis as Henry Morton Stanley in Africa.

He insisted on one thing, which later proved to be not such a bad idea: we had to bring food from Zurich. Our provisions were raw oatmeal, sweetened condensed milk, dried apricots and chocolate. Then there were the sleeping bags, cooking pots, waxed matches and two sets of clothes, as well as regular mountain gear consisting of rope, ice axes and other items. The inclusion of ice axes may seem strange, but the mountains of Corsica are about 8,000 feet tall, and at Easter time there is about the same amount of snow and ice as there is in the high mountains of Norway in summer.

We were given all our provisions on credit by the lovely grocery shop owner in Zurich.[1] You might say she played the same part in our expedition as Ellef Ringnes had done for Fridtjof Nansen's at the time.

---

1 Franchescetti, in Rämistrasse.

At the eleventh hour we acquired an addition to the expedition – George's younger brother, Max, who was studying something or other in Bern. (Why these two boys from South Australia had been placed in Switzerland to study has always been a mystery to me. One that has never been solved.)

As we already have one person named Max in this book, it is just not suitable to have another, but one cannot simply for the sake of overview conjure up new names. That would result in the book's losing its character of serious literature and fall into the category of the kind of writing that does not need to stick to the truth.

We made an agreement with Max that if he could finance his own trip, he would meet us on a certain day in a village we found on the map in the middle of the northern part of Corsica. We gave him the task of bringing a tent he would borrow from the Akademischer Alpenclub (Academic Alpine Club).

Interlude in Italy

The journey from Zurich to the north of Italy does not present any difficulties. Quite the contrary – the express Berlin–Rome train passes through Zurich. If the traveller wishes to admire nature, he can use the day train and alternate between a comfortable saloon car and the dining car; if he does not so wish, he can spend the night in a first-class sleeping car and have his coffee served in bed in the vicinity of Genoa.

George and I decided on another train. It left Zurich very early in the morning and would bring us as far as the Italian border. By changing trains two more times, if everything went according to plan, we would reach Genoa by eleven o'clock at night. How things would proceed from there was temporarily unknown.

The annoying thing about the route we had chosen was that it was necessary to make so many changes and each time we had to buy new tickets. Sometimes third and sometimes fourth class. George took over the purchase of tickets and, after having witnessed this transaction once, I kept my distance.

It is possible that George at that time was not a worthy, or typical, representative of South Australia. It is also possible that what we call 'standing-in-line behaviour' – which looks to be the most amiable part of European culture – was not a just measurement of a continent's cultural level, or its people. But one thing is certain: in this regard George stood at a basic, albeit very effective, level.

His approach to lining up was simple. Loaded with rope and backpack and with his ice axe in his left hand, he went to the very front of the line. Then with the help of the ice axe handle he pushed aside the first three or four customers, glowered at those who were displeased, and placed himself in front of the ticket window, seeing to it that his ice axe protected him from an attack from the rear. Even the patient Swiss, who have had to become accustomed to many strange things on the part of foreign tourists, had a tendency to growl at this tactic, and it was therefore not without reason that I found it prudent to keep my distance each time he used it on the more hot-blooded Italians. But he escaped unharmed. The people probably assumed he was demented – something that coincides with the general opinion about tourists in Italy.

It was pitch dark long before we arrived in Genoa, and it turned out that we had to take a long break there. The situation was that the train going south that corresponded with ours was a sleeping car train without third or fourth class – this did not suit the expedition's finances. The next suitable train did not leave until around four o'clock in the morning, so we had about five hours at our disposal.

My suggestion that we should spend these five hours resting in the station's waiting room was immediately voted down by George, who thought we should use the time to get the best possible insight into the more shady sides of Genoa's nightlife. I was really very much against this because my knowledge of George's aggressive nature led me to believe that night hours spent according to his plan would bring us into unpleasant conflicts.

Here I need to give a little view of Genoa's geography as it appeared to us at that time. The town stretched along the half-circle of a bay and was constructed uphill in the terrain, approximately like an amphitheatre. A big main street ran parallel to the seashore and formed a kind of demarcation between the port area below and the rest of the town above. The train station was at the western end of the main street. The reason I mention these aspects of Genoa is that when I visited some twenty years later while on a car trip, I could not find any of the places or streets I thought I remembered from George's and my visit. Well, a town may change a lot in twenty years, and it is also possible that at either one or both of these occasions I was not at all in Genoa, but in one or several other towns – it is no longer important. For George and me, Genoa was then our night quarters.

First we needed food and drink. That was a simple problem except for our outfits, which made it natural to choose a robust kind of place. We were travelling the whole time dressed in quite dirty and patched sports clothes whose plutocratic origins (Burberry) only an experienced businessman could have detected. We had huge hobnail boots on our feet. If we had not worn them on our feet, we would have had to carry them on our backs, and in other words would have been carrying a double weight.

This may sound paradoxical, but a brief reflection will show that this is correct. While marching one boot will always rest on the ground – in other words, one never carries more than one boot. If, for example, one marches one kilometre in ten minutes with the boots in the backpack, one would carry two boots for ten minutes in order to get them from one place to another, while with the boots on one's feet one would carry each boot for just five minutes – which amounts to one boot for ten minutes.

How both boots nevertheless reach their destination remains quite mysterious and the theoretical treatment of the problem has throughout time posed serious problems for physicists.[1] No satisfying explanation having been found without dismissing the principles on which our present-day physics are based; I maintain that the case has not been attributed sufficient attention.[2] In reality it is mainly of interest to walkers, and here one must pay attention to the problem having been taken up by science, but only after the advent of the age of the automobile.

Well, we soon found an excellent pub, where our attire perhaps brought some polite interest, but no offence in any way.

In general, the farther one gets from the north, the less such conventional things as clothing are important. In tropical areas

---

1   See also Professor Sahulka, 'Beiträge zur Beleuchtung der scheinbaren Wiederspruches in der Vektoranalyse intermittierenden Lasttragens', *Annalen der Physik*, 1905: 422.

2   With the exception of Arthur Eddington, who in his work *New Aspects of Gravitational Problems* presents a new and very radical theory that would be too far-fetched to get into here.

one must dress and behave most peculiarly before heads turn in the street. But everyone knows the story about the man who was walking in Piccadilly in a morning coat with only one button done up instead of two. He was incarcerated for having caused a riot.

The same is the case of the so-called places of 'annoying necessity'. To make a necessary visit when nature calls of strictly banal character in the northern countries, one must usually go underground into a facility that has cost 200,000 kroner and which is covered in porcelain tiles. In addition, it costs ten øre, a considerable sum for gentlemen with a prostate condition.

In France and northern Italy, the situation is simpler and cheaper; and at approximate forty-degree latitude, they have converted to a practical system consisting of placing a plaque on a suitable building where this simple business is concluded with one's back end facing the public. (Farther south, the users may be facing the other way – what do I know?)

I think this is preferable over the Nordic system, which is too strict and also indicates a poorly reasoned recognition of the northerners' opposition to exhibitionism.

Think of London, for example – I remember living there once with a Norwegian friend who would later become a highly venerated judge in Oslo. One afternoon he returned to the boarding house, shaken to the core by something he had seen painted on a wall. (It was just the kind of wall where in the south it would have been obvious to follow a call of nature.)

'I had no idea,' he said, 'that the situation in England was still so barbaric. One has to hope it is a misunderstanding that it is still there.'

On the wall in big black letters had been written, 'Anybody doing nuisance on this wall will be immediately prosecuted.' One would never have found anything like it on an Italian wall.

The only annoying thing that happened at the pub, where we ate macaroni and drank wine, was that the waiter refused to accept our counterfeit money. It did not help to insist that we had had it exchanged at the railroad station – we had to pay with real money.

The main street was still lit up when we came out of the pub. It was a little past midnight and now George had to study the nightlife in the port area to find where he thought there was the best chance of finding some entertainment.

Personally I have always been against throwing myself unnecessarily into warlike involvements. Mostly my attitude toward war is the same as that of Johan Herman Wessel, who so beautifully expressed his sentiment in his poem about Saint Sebastian:

I love Peace
And think War is always Wretched
Perhaps I would think War more lovely
Were I as brave as I am honest.

After wandering around a little we found a cellar pub just above the main street that separated the port area from the rest of the town. There we joined the company of some quite shabby persons of dubious nationality who were playing billiards for money.

We did not succeed in finding a common language. The billiard players gave the impression of knowing four or five different ones from the eastern Mediterranean, but it was not possible to reach any closer contact than Italian. George and I were relegated to a small phrasebook, published by Baedeker, in which it was never possible to find anything resembling what we really wanted to say.

When you play billiards for money and want to know what the wager is, it won't do to ask, '*Wie viel kostet das Zimmer? Qanto costa questa camera?* (How much is the room?)' We wouldn't understand the response anyway and answer according to the book: '*E troppo cara; mostramo una meno camera.* (That is too expensive, show me a smaller room.)'

It was somewhat of a miracle that we nevertheless solved the situation and managed to start some sort of gamble involving billiards.

The game was played with a large number of balls and a dish of money in the middle of the billiard table. Every time a player turned the dish over, the others shared the money. Here, George thought, was an opportunity to use the fake silver coins we had brought with us. He figured that even if we lost about twice as much as we won, this would be a winning proposition. There was not much light in the cellar and his speculation seemed therefore to be of sound foundation.

We did well for a while. True, we did lose some of the large silver coins we had brought, but on the other hand got quite a few others back and saw to it that we got smaller coins that we knew were more valuable. Apparently no one took particular notice of the kind of money they were winning from us, but it was clear that in the long run, this could not continue. I finally succeeded in convincing George to end this game while the going was still good. We quietly snuck out of the place while our players were busy in an animated discussion about some technical detail of the play.

It was a little past two when we came into the street again and the town seemed deserted. I suggested that we go back to the station and wait for our train and George was at first inclined to agree to this reasonable suggestion, although he was very disappointed in what Genoa nightlife had to offer in terms of excitement.

He was wrong about the nightlife. When we were about 300 feet away from the pub, three of our earlier friends from the billiards game came into the street, very agitated and gesticulating. There was no mistaking their wish to join us again.

Under these circumstances I found it even more natural to get back to the station by the shortest possible route. It was probably related to my guilty conscience about the distribution of counterfeit money. But George was of the opposite opinion: here he finally saw an opportunity to experience something.

From the main street where we now found ourselves, a number of small, narrow alleys went down toward the port area. Most of them started with a few steps down from the street's southern pavement. George thought this was the right terrain.

I was in a difficult situation. It wasn't easy to know what was the riskiest – to separate from George or to follow him. I chose the latter and we went down one of the stairs toward the port alleys.

Not far behind us came the three billiard players. Two were big, one was small.

'It is clear,' I said to George, 'that they have not come to bid us a fond farewell.'

George was also aware of this. He looked brightly to the future.

'Well,' he said, 'if we're going to have a fight with three people down here – people who are well known in the area and probably use knives – it is just as well that we start things. The element of surprise is not to be underestimated.'

We went to the right at the nearest street corner and waited. Right by the corner stood a dirty gas light that barely illuminated the closest few feet around it. Our battle plan, according to my suggestion, was that George would take on the two big ones and I the small one. George thought this was fine.

As far as the element of surprise was concerned, I am sure it was present. When the three of them showed up around the corner, the first one (one of the big ones) received, without a trace of prior debate, a solid uppercut from George, while I, who lately had tried to specialise in jiu-jitsu, started in on the small one.

Someone who is completely unprepared and who has no idea of jiu-jitsu does not have a chance against a sudden attack when it is executed with sufficient brutality, and my opponent (if one could call him that, for he made no opposition) was lying in the street within a few seconds, where I too found myself due to my clumsiness, as I stumbled over him when he fell. Unlike him, I had not hit the back of my head on the cobblestones, and I got back on my feet quite quickly. My opponent – or rather my victim – was lying completely still.

When I looked to see what George was up to, I saw that he had grabbed the gas light with his left hand and the second of the billiard players by the hair with his right hand. At short intervals he was banging the back of the man's head against the gas light.

After each bang, the billiard player sank down a little and gradually went from a sitting and then to a prone position.

The first one that George had become acquainted with had by then regained his feet. For a moment he looked at the remains of his two friends and then quickly resorted to flight-like retreat. The two remaining ones stayed completely still. It was what one might characterise as an annihilating battle.

'Now,' I said to George, 'I think it would be best if we follow my original suggestion and find the station as quickly as possible. First of all, we can count on the third guy soon being back with reinforcements, and second, I think it looks bad for those who are lying here. God only knows if they'll revive!'

For once George agreed, and after stumbling around a little in the now-empty port area, we finally found our way back to the main street and reached the station half an hour before our train was to leave.

I think it was a relief even for George when we finally had put Genoa behind us and were being jostled toward Pisa, where we once again would change trains to reach the port of Livorno.

Just before we reached Pisa, George, who was sitting opposite me, woke up. 'Bryn,' he said, 'it was noble of you to let me have the two big ones. I'll never forget that.'

'My dear,' I said, 'don't mention it.'

Pisa, which we reached in the morning, is generally known for its leaning tower, and among people who pretend to have a classical or scientific education, the tower is also known for Galileo Galilei's dealings with it. As we know, Galilei allegedly used the leaning tower to construct one of his many heretical theories, the one about bodies of different masses falling at equal speed in a vacuum.

We had a few hours to wait for our train to Livorno and set out in full gear into town and the big Piazza del Duomo, where the Campanile and other points of interest reside. The plan was basically first to go up into the tower in a normal way and look at the view, but the tower was closed; the guard who demanded one lira from tourists to let them in did not arrive until ten o'clock.

This was, in reality, a stroke of luck. Already at this point in time, the horrible practice had been instituted of gathering up a suitable group of innocent tourists and hauling them around through such historical monuments with a so-called guide, who in a hectoring manner rattles off a memorised lecture that has something to do with the monument, but never about something one has an interest in currently. I have on various later occasions been exposed to this curse on the travelling public; this curse for which even the Inquisition's most crafty torture would be altogether too mild a punishment.

It is obvious that these tour guides are driven by a malignant form of sadism. Not even promises of an increased honorarium can make them keep quiet about the chair which seated such and such a king or queen on some long-forgotten, insignificant occasion.

Only once have I seen a guide of this kind knocked out. It was a wonderful experience. With some French friends I was visiting a French castle, known for its old tapestries. We had successfully escaped from the flock of guided sheep and were having a nice, quiet time. But then we were discovered and the guide, who probably thought we had escaped too lightly, threw himself on us with a recitation about the history of the tapestry factory.

My French host, a distinguished, older gentleman, looked seriously at the guide and said: '*Désistez, cher monsieur, je vous en supplie, je suis sourd et en outre je ne comprends pas un mot de votre langue.* (Desist, dear sir, I am deaf and furthermore I do not understand a word of your language.)'

The guide shook his head and thereafter followed us at a polite distance. His conviction that we were dangerous and strange was not diminished by the fact that he was given an extra tip when we parted ways.

However, this was not what preoccupied me and George – George especially. George thought this was an opportune moment to climb the north face of the leaning tower, the least steep side.

I was doubtful about this enterprise, mostly because I thought it might disturb the local Pisans' patriotic sentiments and bring us into unwanted conflict with enforcers of the law. But George is not the kind who lets such petty concerns put a brake on his desire to act. He organised a camp on the north end of Piazza del Duomo, took off his hobnail boots, put on tennis shoes and attacked the leaning tower. He brought with him only an ice axe, which the study of the tower's façade had shown to be necessary.

I stayed in camp. I told George it was in order to guard our equipment, but my thought was also toward the expedition's future, and how it would be beneficial for both its members not to be arrested at the same time.

Scaling the leaning tower is fundamentally different from scaling a normal house wall. The tower is constructed of a number of circular balconies with richly sculpted railing and thick, smooth marble columns which, along with the railing, form the outer façade. The columns are too thick to be used as climbing poles, and the distance from the upper edge of the railing to the frieze on the underside of the next one is too great to be within the reach of the hands of even a tall man. This was where the ice axe was useful. When George stood on a railing close to a column he could get the tip of the ice axe into an opening in the railing of the balcony above. Squeezing his legs around the column and getting a hold on the ice axe with his right hand, he managed to scoot up until he had a hold with both hands and could lift himself up. It was quite a nice accomplishment.

So thought many members of Pisa's young male population who, far from being angry over the assault on the cultural monument, encouraged George with increasingly fiery shouts.

That's how it went all the way to the fourth floor. But then came what I had feared – the enforcers of the law. At first they also took it nicely and were satisfied to be part of the interested audience. But then some citizen or other must have alerted them to the fact that something was happening that ran counter to morals and the public order. They walked over to the foot of the tower and started to holler in an unmistakable fashion.

George also must have heard the false note that had mingled with the encouraging shouts, for he turned and looked down before he was about to start on the next landing. The two constables shouted many things at him, probably a reasonable choice of abusive words that constables in Italy employ toward miscreants caught red-handed, but this did not help in the case of George, whose knowledge of the Italian language was severely limited.

George did understand that he needed tools to help him out, so he pulled a phrasebook out of his pocket as he straddled the railing. After a short period of study he found something he obviously thought would suit the situation and addressed the officers of the law: '*Sono per la prima volta in Italia.* (This is my first time in Italy.)' And then: '*Viaggio per ristabilirmi.* (I am travelling for my health.)'

That clearly must have convinced the officers of the law, as well as the public, that he was crazy, something that from their point of view was not so difficult to explain, and the discussion died down.

Satisfied with the results of his linguistic exercise, George started up to the fifth level, which he reached accompanied by an almost admiring public mumble.

There is every reason to believe that he would have reached the top and thereby have accomplished the ascent of the leaning tower from the north, had not the tower guard shown up in the meantime.

His view of George's endeavour was strictly mathematical. He regarded it as a cowardly attempt to avoid the entry fee, and along with the two constables he reached the fifth floor just as George was about to continue. The trip came to an end and George had to pay one lira, as if he were just an ordinary visitor.

Another twelve to fifteen years would go by before the climbing of walls and tower façades became not just a very popular but also highly paid sport.[3]

George performed many successful ascents of façades during the rest of our expedition. In general he had difficulty keeping passive if an opportunity to do something or other presented itself. And this characteristic did not diminish over time – to the contrary, one might even say. It must have been fifteen or twenty years later that he conducted the first ascent of the south-east corner of the white ballroom behind the palm gardens of Oslo's Grand Hotel.

---

3 In this regard it may be of note that the first ascent of the leaning tower from the north was accomplished by an Italian around 1925. The ascent was filmed.

By then he was a professor and had just given a lecture to the Norwegian Alpine Club about the first Mount Everest expedition. One of the other participants also reached the roof but then made the mistake of jumping off backwards – he was probably longing for a drink – and broke the heels of both his feet. A typical victim of the subjective dangers of climbing.

After the attack on the leaning tower had thus been repelled, we planned a trip to Pisa's other points of interest, but after a while had to give up because of the ever-increasing crowd of hopeful Pisa youths, who with lively shouts encouraged us to new endeavours.

We retreated in good order to the railroad station, where we still had a few hours to wait before the next train would bring us to Livorno.

Livorno was our last stop on the European mainland. It is, or, at any rate, was at that time, known mainly for its chicken farms and had through generations been the home of 'White Italians'. When this breed, created by Giordani Bruno, was supposedly introduced by Francis Bacon to England under Queen Elizabeth's reign, the English noticed that it distinguished itself from other breeds of chicken by its spurs, which were located unusually high up on its legs. In England this breed of chicken got the name 'Leghorn' and, as if that weren't enough, the town of Livorno was also given this name, which it has never been able to shed.

I think this is one of the worst examples of the arrogance with which foreign place and personal names have been treated through time.

Life on board

The trip from Livorno to the port of Bastia in Corsica takes six to eight hours by boat. It is a cheap trip when one travels on deck, and that's what George and I did.

The boat was small and the swells made by a fresh northerly wind made it roll in a way that neither of us liked, but we didn't say anything about it to one another. On the contrary, when some time had passed without feeling undisputable signs of seasickness, we became quite cheerful and told true or imagined stories about earlier exploits on the waves.

I say true or imagined because it may very well be that George's stories were true. George had, so he said, travelled for six weeks of consecutive storms with a sailing vessel from Australia to Europe. He had spent the best part of the day climbing the rigging and at certain intervals he went down and stood upside down in the head, although this did not prevent him from enjoying great quantities of pork and peas several times a day.

These were feats I could not easily compete with, but I mentioned that it was generally true that you didn't become seasick on sailing vessels, for steamships were worse; they lurched in a different way. Just have a try with the masts here, for example. One word followed the next as they say, and at the end there was no way around it. I was to tie my handkerchief at the top of the foremast and George his at the top of the mainmast, and then we would change places and bring them back down.

Going up went quite well. First up the shrouds to the lower crosstree, followed by fifteen to eighteen feet on a rope to the higher one, and then easy climbing with the help of the flag line to the top. It was when I came down to the lower crosstree again that I began to feel unwell. It was made like a kind of platform and the shrouds ended under it so that you had to lie on your stomach and feel your way with your feet to find the top rung. I looked down and shouldn't have done that. Sometimes I had the deck under me and sometimes the sea, first on one and then the other side of the ship. I was suddenly convinced that it was physically impossible to get down. But what then?

The exercise was witnessed with interest and something almost resembling respect by the crew, and if I now asked for help I would lose face once and for all, not just in front of the crew but in front of George as well. Oh, George, how was he faring?

I looked over at the mainmast. George was sitting there on the lower crosstree at about the same height as me and his handkerchief waved from the top of the mast.

'Hello,' I said, 'it's nice here. I think I'll stay up here for a while and enjoy the view.'

'That's what I think too,' he said, 'it would be a shame to go down to the dirty deck again.'

We sat like that for about a half an hour, and if I am to judge by how I felt, we were not having a good time.

The rolling of the ship diminished after a while and with a terrific effort of will and muscles I succeeded in getting down to the shroud and on down to the deck. George came down shortly thereafter. He thought I looked a little pale, but didn't expand on the theme after I made him take a look at himself in the mirror. The fresh air I had enjoyed on the foremast had at short intervals been mixed with thick sooty smoke from the stack back where he was. He said it was so nice up there that he hadn't noticed.

After a suitable rest we were sufficiently restituted to fortify ourselves with bread, cheese and wine. We then we spread our sleeping bags out on the deck and went to sleep with our heads on our backpacks.

In the afternoon we arrived in Bastia and set our hobnail boots on Corsican soil.

A short review
of Corsica's history

George and I had no knowledge of Corsica's history and geography other than being aware that it was Napoleon's birthplace and that there was a series of high mountains, among which several that had not been scaled.

Many people may be inclined to criticise us for starting out on such a meaningful expedition without first conducting studies of an historical or geographical nature. By reading about similar expeditions you get the impression that their leaders spent years of their lives doing just that. Such criticism would be unwarranted. A big part of the pleasure of such exploratory journeys consists of the presence of a subjective lack of knowledge of the places and situations one will encounter. Setting out on a journey of discovery along a route you have previously read a thorough description of in Baedeker does not have the same charm as setting out into what is for you a completely unknown terrain.

It is therefore probably wrong when from reading books about journeys of discovery you get the impression that they have been thoroughly prepared in that regard. Most of them have probably just gone ahead and waited to do the studying later.

Often the worst prepared expeditions become the most successful. A few years before George and I went to Corsica on the aforementioned loose premises, a few of my friends went from Norway to India to climb one of the peaks in the Himalaya they had heard about.

When they arrived there it turned out, first of all, that the mountain in question was located in Nepal, where no foreigner was allowed, and second, that the time of year was exactly the one that was not suitable at all to ascend mountains in the Himalaya.

But that did not stop them in any way. They went on a six-month drinking binge in Ceylon and, fortified by their debauched life, returned to the mountains and climbed another peak, also previously unclimbed, and thereby reached a higher altitude than anyone had before.[1]

Neither George nor I have been recognised by geographical science as the discoverers of Corsica. Also, we have been too reticent to demand such recognition, even though it may have been well deserved. The discovery of a populated country will always be a strictly subjective endeavour. Both Leif Erikson and Columbus separately discovered America. The only difference between them on the one hand, and George and me on the other, was that they did not know what the country was called.

But what I first and foremost want to arrive at here is that the only decidedly necessary condition for discovery is that the explorer himself have no previous knowledge of what he is discovering. That others may have this knowledge cannot be avoided, but this circumstance does not diminish the new discoverer's joy in the research.[2] It is one thing that you yourself have no knowledge about what you are embarking upon; as already mentioned, that is almost a necessary condition for a serious effort of this kind. It's another thing when later you have to make everyone else familiar with the results of the journey, that you may find it reasonable to give a little orientation about things you yourself had refrained from becoming familiar with until later.

Many of the things one experiences during such an expedition thereby, in the light of history, are placed in relief, which otherwise might be missing.

Corsica, as we know, is an island in the Mediterranean Sea, approximately 160 miles long from north to south and approximately eighty miles wide from east to west.

Corsica in bygone days was called Cyrnus, but this was not the

---

1 Carl Wilhelm Rubenson and Ingvald Monrad-Aas' ascent of Kabru (23,900 feet) in 1907.

2 See also Professor Leacock's work, *My Discovery of England*, which was published in Canada as late as 1924.

island's original name. Originally its name was Corsica; it was named after one of Hercules' many illegitimate sons, Corsus, who, with his brother Sardus, discovered Corsica and Sardinia while on a journey.[3]

Other than this event, we hear little about Corsica before the Phoenicians began to colonise the island about five to six hundred years before the birth of Christ. It was at that time that the Corsicans' fight for freedom started. (To what extent it is now over is not easy to know; it was still going on in the 1930s.)

There must have been people on Corsica[4] long before the Phoenicians arrived. The inhabitants have always resisted all who have wanted to conquer the island. The battles regularly resulted in the inhabitants retreating to the mountains, while the conquerors stayed in the coastal areas until they were slaughtered or replaced by other conquerors.

After the Phoenicians came the Etruscans, the Cretans, the Carthaginians and then, of course, the Romans, who essentially used Corsica as a place of disappearance for people who for one reason or another had made themselves less than popular.

Around the time of the birth of Christ one might say that a Corsican nation had developed, composed of the original population and the more robust elements of the Phoenician, Greek and Carthaginian colonists. From this period we have a description of Corsicans by Seneca, the well-known Roman philosopher who spent eight years in exile on the island, apparently because he had behaved toward Messalina about the same way Joseph behaved toward Potifar's wife.

---

3 Another version regarding the origin of the name Corsica can be found in *Histoire de la Corse* by Pierre-Paul Raoul Colonna de Cesari-Rocca and Louis Villat (Boivin et Cie, Paris, 1916). That version goes as follows: a Ligurian woman saw a calf swim out to sea and come back fat and full. The next time, she swam with the calf, came to an island and later told friends and family about it. The Ligurians (who surely belong to Corsica's earliest immigrants) travelled to the island and named it after the woman, whose name was Corsa.

In my opinion, this version cannot be taken seriously. One must not forget that the shortest distance from the Ligurian coast (south of France) to Corsica is about 110 miles; and even though one should not deny the possibility of a woman at that time being able to swim such a distance, it is completely unthinkable that a calf could have returned fat after having done so.

4 Probably Ligurians.

Seneca was not particularly pleased with his stay and the company: 'Where does one find,' Seneca writes, 'anything as naked and torn as this land of cliffs? Where does one find a land more deprived of products – where the people are less welcoming, whose location is sadder and whose climate more inhospitable?'

And about the Corsicans especially he declares epigram-matically: '*Prima est ulcisci lex, altera vivere raptu, tertia mentiri, quarta negare deos.* (Their first is to execute the law, the next to live in pleasure, the third to lie, the fourth to deny the gods.)' Generally nice qualities, as one can see.

After his exile was ended, Seneca became teacher to young Nero, who may of course have been exposed to considerable Corsican influences during his childhood years.

During and after the fall of Rome, Corsica was visited by a succession of Cimbri, Vandals and Turks. None of these gained any long-term dominance on the island but it goes without saying that they left numerous illegitimate children, thereby contributing to the enhancement of the race.

In the course of these centuries, the Corsicans developed into a very contentious nation. They were practically always engaged in fighting. As a rule the situation was such that four or five large districts would fight each other under their respective leaders, whenever the island was not as a whole being subjected to an invasion from the outside.

Inside each of the districts there were a series of communities or villages, and if the whole district was not in a conflict with one or more of the others, the communities and villages within the district fought each other.

On the rare occasion when not even one community was in conflict with one or more other communities, one contented oneself with the perpetual conflict between individual families, organised in Corsica so that it can never end once it has started. The conflict begins when a young man from one family seduces a girl from another, or proposes to her and is refused. This then automatically leads to the seducer being killed by the girl's brother, or to the slighted suitor killing the brother. The tradition that developed demanded that any murder of a family member must be settled by the murder of at least two members of the murderer's family – it is easy to see how these vendettas progressed.

The peculiar thing, from a mathematician's point of view, is that there is anyone left at all. But that must be attributed to their practically always being occupied with fighting people more or less from the outside, and therefore not finding time to consistently carry out the vendetta. That almost became a form of entertainment in leisure times.

Around the year AD 1000, Corsica came into conflict with external enemies, and this struggle continued with short interruptions into the end of the eighteenth century, although the enemy was not always the same. This period of unrest was introduced by Pope Gregory VII, who decided that Christianity was to be instituted in Corsica, and to that end gave the island to the archbishops of Pisa and Genoa to hold in common.

The Corsicans immediately put their internal strife aside and took up the fight against their new owners. The fight was principally against the Genoese, since the Genoese immigrants and mercenaries occupied the coastal towns and areas, while the inhabitants kept to the mountains, whence they made their assaults.

In the course of this period, Corsica went through a series of political phases. Around the year AD 1300, for example, came the first organised party akin to Communism. This group, the so-called Giovannali, kept to the mountains around Carbini. The Corsican historian Anton Pietro Filippini tells of this communist sect in which women were equal to men, and its law said that everything was owned in common – women as well as children and property. They multiplied rapidly. (Whether this was by reproduction or by newfound members is not apparent from Filippini's account.)

Considering that all this took place some 600 years ago, one cannot say that the development on a socio-political level moves with particular speed.

The Giovannali family was after a time eradicated by order of the Pope, who at that time lived in Avignon and hired French troops for the job.

One of the most picturesque and certainly most typical of Corsican characters from this long period of struggle was Sampiero, who lived in the sixteenth century. Sampiero was a Corsican from the mountain area who early on went into foreign war service. Among other things, he served the house of Medici and later became the leader of a Corsican regiment under François I of France. In 1547 he came back to Corsica as an adult, and there he married a Corsican woman from a very good family. He later killed the lady, Vanina d'Ornano, when he discovered that in his absence she had made plans to travel to Genoa.

At the time of Sampiero, Corsica had been transferred to the Genoese state bank for the sum of 2,000 gold scudi. Sampiero took up the fight against the mercenaries that the Genoese bank kept in Corsica. He succeeded in driving the Genoese troops away from almost the entire island, but they received reinforcements and Sampiero was driven out in 1559, betrayed by his own followers.

Now Sampiero again went into foreign war service, to Algeria and Turkey among other places, but came back to Corsica once again in 1564 with forty-three men. He succeeded in quickly gathering some of his old followers, and he beat the Genoese troops in two battles – one near Corte and one near Vescovato – and then the war was on again in all seriousness.

The Genoese sent an army of several thousand German and Italian mercenaries under its best commander, Stephan Doria. According to the story, Stephan Doria was not only the most competent but also one of the cruellest commanders – and this in an era when such commanders were legion. According to Gregorovius's[5] book on Corsican history, Doria himself is supposed to have given the following summary of his principles of war:

'When the Athenians occupied Melos after seven months of resistance, they killed all inhabitants over fourteen years old and subsequently sent a colony of their own to populate the city again.

---

5 Ferdinand Gregorovius, *Corsica* (Leipzig: Bernina Verlag, 1936).

Why shouldn't we follow the Athenian example? Should the Corsicans deserve less punishment than the rebels of Melos? By using these terrible punishments, the Athenians wanted to accomplish the conquest of the Peloponnese, all of Greece, Africa, Italy and Sicily. By killing all their enemies, they re-established respect and fear of their weapons.

It will be said that we, by exterminating the population, have violated all the laws of humanity and civilisation. But what does that matter if they will only fear us? That is all I demand. I put more weight on Genoa's judgment than on that of posterity, which one in vain tries to frighten me with. This empty word – posterity – hampers only the weak and indecisive. It is in our interest to broaden the scope of our conquests and deprive the rebels of everything that may be helpful in war. There are only three ways: ruin the harvest, burn the villages and destroy the towers where they are entrenched when they must retreat.'

On the basis of what has been said, Doria was quite an angel compared to Sampiero, and it is easy to imagine that the situation in Corsica during this war was not particularly idyllic.

Sampiero finally succeeded in striking Doria a decisive defeat, as a result of which he went back to Italy, though the Genoese still ruled the coastal towns and the areas around them. In 1567, traitors succeeded in luring Sampiero into an ambush and killed him. Sampiero is one of two Corsican heroes. (The other is not Napoleon.)

The Corsicans continued the war after Sampiero's death, and a few hundred years later in the mid-eighteenth century, in connection with the war, a strange event took place and Corsica suddenly became a kingdom.

This happened when the German baron Theodor von Neuhof, a well-known adventurer at that time, arrived with a shipload of guns and ammunition, which he traded to the Corsican freedom fighters in return for being nominated king, which he became. King Theodor's short-lived reign (it lasted approximately five months) can unquestionably be characterised as Corsica's period of glory as far as titles are concerned. When he left after five months to go to Amsterdam with the intention of borrowing money, the Corsican army had five marshals and about thirty commanding generals. There were a comparable number of officers, but soldiers were in short supply. The heads of all the big families had been named dukes and had received the great cross of the newly established Corsican order Della Liberazione. The heads of the lesser families had become marquis and only a few insignificant persons in King Theodor's entourage had to content themselves with becoming mere counts.

After King Theodor had left, the Corsicans continued their lives and their strife without being bothered by titles. Finally the Genoese grew tired of them and sold Corsica to the French in 1768.

At this time Corsica had for many years been under the leadership of Pasquale Paoli, who along with Sampiero is the most popular figure in the history of the island. To Paoli and his Corsican supporters, the sale to France had no other significance than changing the enemy, and the struggle continued. The new enemy was stronger than the old one and Paoli suffered a decisive defeat in 1769.

Among Paoli's closest comrades-in-arms was Carlo Buonaparte, who after Paoli's defeat went over to the enemy and joined the French governor Marboeuf. This had decidedly broader ramifications than Carlo had probably anticipated, for it was in return for the favours he performed for Marboeuf that the latter got Carlo's son Nabulio into the military academy in Brienne. Thereafter, as we know, it did not take long before Nabulio, under his *nom de guerre* Napoleon, began to modernise Europe's borders and dynasties. It is also interesting to remember that at the same time Nabulio was growing up in Ajaccio there was a common solider in Bastia's French Regiment, Jean Bernadotte, who also achieved a great career – whether because of or in spite of marrying Buonaparte's earlier fiancée, Désirée Clary, it is not clear.

Whatever the opinion about him and his later switch to France and Napoleon's enemies, he is in any case the only son from the petite bourgeoisie from that period to end up being the progenitor of a lasting legitimate dynasty.

Corsica's history after Napoleon's time has not been marked by any momentous events. In 1848, Louis Napoleon was elected Corsica's deputy to the National Assembly, and in other ways Corsicans have managed to make a lot of mischief. The Corsican bandits – the only part of the population to preserve the distinctive traits of the people and to honour the old traditions – have conducted a practically uninterrupted war against the French authorities, not because they were French, but because they were authorities. As late as 1931 there were regular battles with tanks and considerable numbers of troops in the mountain regions around Monte Rotondo.[6]

---

6 This short review of Corsica's history does not claim to be complete or original. For those who want further immersion in the material, I can refer them to the sources I have used.

Bastia and Capo Corso

As I said, we set our hobnailed boots on Corsican soil and were immediately assaulted by an indeterminate number of ragged youths, who not only offered to carry our luggage but also gave the definite impression of having the right to do so. It was good luck that we had the ice axe along; in general it is a piece of equipment that comes in handy both here and there.

Thanks to the ice axe and George's furious comments, whose meaning one could hardly misunderstand even without any knowledge of the Australian language, we got away from the pier and started up toward the town centre, followed at a respectful distance, but as far as I could judge, without respectful comments, by the disappointed mass of dissatisfied porters.

About Bastia one could say as one would about Mandal: it is not a big town, but even so it is the biggest in Corsica. Nor is it a Corsican town; it was constructed by the Genoese at the end of the fourteenth century and takes its name from the *bastione* the Genoese established during their many hundreds of years of struggle against the Corsicans. Until 1811 it was nominally the Corsican capital, but then had to cede its place to Ajaccio – probably because this was Napoleon's birthplace – while Bastia had nothing to recommend it, if one may be permitted to say so, other than the crown prince of Sweden, Bernadotte, who had toiled there for a few years as a soldier.

The town of Bastia is situated in approximately the same way as Genoa, around an excellent harbour, which offers little room for construction. It therefore distinguishes itself by a series of tall buildings which have come about by new buildings being added on top of the old ones as the need for more room arose. You therefore come upon buildings where the three or four lower floors are four to five hundred years old, while the upper ones are several hundred years younger and hence of another kind of style.

The buildings are constructed of bad stone and chalk. This fact is in and of itself noteworthy, considering that in Corsica there is a rich choice of fine sorts of stone. The street pavement surface, however, is marble throughout, although this is difficult to ascertain because of the extremely basic cleaning facilities.

Down by the harbour is a big open square, Place Saint-Nicolas, and in the middle a statue of Napoleon I. The statue bears no resemblance to Napoleon, neither in the way of looks nor clothing. It mostly resembles Nero. So far as we know, Napoleon has never been to Bastia.

Bastia has a series of hotels that make a great impression, at least so far as their names are concerned: Imperial Palace, Hotel de France, Hotel de l'Europe and Hotel de l'Univers. We did not choose any of these, instead booking into a humble inn, named after the freedom hero Paoli. We thought that would suit the expedition's finances.

The Paoli hostel was a pub of the simpler sort, with a few serviceable guestrooms above and a cafe with billiards on the first floor. I cannot deny that the sight of the billiard table made me a little worried about the future, and this proved to be not unwarranted.

After a tasty and cheap dinner consisting of a *bouillabaisse*-like soup and spaghetti, we settled down in the pub. We were the only guests, and were entertained by the innkeeper. Of course George had to bring the conversation around to billiards, which unfortunately the innkeeper was also very interested in. It was not long before George, who had a high opinion of my abilities as a billiard player, managed to arrange a match between the innkeeper and me.

Our host explained that the billiard table was at the free disposal of his guests, albeit on the condition that they must pay in case they poke a hole in the billiard cloth. The fee, he explained, was ten francs for the first hole and five for each of the following. The billiard table was not one of those on which you play a championship: the pockets were hard as rocks and the balls made of some sort of strange inelastic material rubbed in fat, obviously applied so that the cue would slip and slash the billiard cloth. The billiard cloth closely resembled a patchwork quilt, something we might have seen had the light been better. There was hardly a spot as big as an inch square where the cloth hadn't been torn and then fastened to the support with spit or other adhesive.

After an hour of playing I had soundly trounced the innkeeper and George had won his bet of ten francs. But when our host then came with an extra lamp to examine the billiard cloth, it had seventeen gashes, making for ninety francs. This was not good business for the expedition, even though we figured we could use the counterfeit money we had in reserve.

This was where George showed himself to be a leader of strategic abilities. He slapped our host on the shoulder, offered him a drink and explained that we planned to be there for some time, so the balance due to the inn could be added to the bill. Fortunately, there were at that time still gullible innkeepers. We retired to our room in good order without having been made to pay compensation for the gashes. At about four thirty the next morning we eased down a double rope from our window on the third floor and started out on our hike to Capo Corso. On the table in our room we left money (fake) to cover room and board, but saved the expense of the billiards.

There was a little discussion between George and me about this. George was mostly inclined to leave the premises without any kind of payment, thinking that would be suitable punishment for our host's obvious cheating with the billiard cloth. My point of view was that before we left we should ensure that we would not later be caught as hotel swindlers, and George finally agreed, though it certainly was against his conviction.

Capo Corso is a long spit of land that stretches from Bastia approximately thirty miles north. At its widest, it stretches about seven miles. Along the middle of the spit of land there is a kind of mountain range, whose highest point, Cima delle Folicce, lies roughly 4,200 feet above sea level.

We knew nothing about Capo Corso and had decided to take a few days to find out if there were any peaks of interest to mountain climbers, while at the same time gaining some experience with our equipment's suitability for overnight use in mountain areas. On the trip north we kept to the country road along the east coast and experienced nothing. We had brought quite a bit of luggage along, since for good reasons we had not found it wise to leave anything at the hotel.

It was heavy and hard going north at the crack of dawn through groves of chestnuts and palms. Every once in a while we passed old cemeteries with the only marble structures we ever saw in Corsica.

Around dinnertime we had reached a little village, Marine del Porticciolo, about twenty miles from Bastia and a little north of the highest part of the mountain chain on Capo Corso. We bought bread and chestnuts and turned west up a little valley in order to get up to the higher part of the mountain ridge. When we had come away from the coast a little, it started to pour down with rain. We had not yet reached the mountain areas, so we walked around a pasture where there was a quite ordinary barn. We settled down there and prepared a substantial meal combining lunch and dinner. There was ample good, dry hay in the barn, and we had no difficulty convincing each other to stay the night and wait for the weather to clear up.

When we stepped out the next morning we could establish two things: first of all, that the weather had become nice, and second, that a flock of curious people had gathered at a suitable distance from our lodgings. Someone had probably seen the light from our lamps the night before. Even in this peaceful part of Corsica the population was quite careful about strangers – experience had probably taught them that.

We were soon talking with them and we did our best to make tourism popular, but we could barely keep a conversation going that was comprehensible to both parties in our respective forms of bad French. Our explanation that we had come from a distant country to go hiking in the high mountains of Corsica could not have seemed particularly convincing, even if they were much too polite to express any doubt about our intentions and our *métier*.

Coils of rope and the ice axes in particular caused much interest. A stout, middle-aged farmer held and weighed one of the ice axes in his hand for a long time while we explained what its use was. Here we were probably approaching the limit of what even a polite and willing audience could accept, and the man, who gave back the ice axe, said that it was probably good for chopping into ice but could certainly be used for other things as well. He concluded with a knowing smile.

That day we went up the ridge just north of the highest peak, Cima delle Folicce. From a mountain climber's point of view, both this peak and the rest of the peaks on Capo Corso were disappointing.

Mountain climbers generally separate mountains into three categories. In the highest class, which incidentally is quite rare, are the peaks that are difficult to ascend at all. The second class, which is the most common, comprises those peaks and mountains that are difficult to ascend from one side or another. The third and lowest class is made up of those mountains it is not difficult to get up, no matter where you go. This third class is of no interest, and it is not easy to find any reasonable explanation why such mountains are made at all.

The mountain chain in Capo Corso belonged to the third class, and the trip back to the area around Bastia consisted of going up and down gentle, rocky slopes.

We spent the next night in the open up on the hill right outside Bastia's built-up area, because we wanted to test our equipment and because we did not find it particularly attractive or advisable to spend the night in town.

The next morning we reached the railroad which goes from Bastia to Calvi and at one of the stations outside of the town we boarded the train.

Valle Tartagine and
Capo al Dente

About halfway between Bastia and Calvi and at the highest point of the railroad line, we had decided that we would start our first expedition into the unknown high country. The mountain valley which was our first goal is called Valle Tartagine. It lies, like most of the mountain valleys there, in an east–west direction and is bordered to the west by a series of peaks that fall steeply down toward the coast.

These peaks are from 6,900–7,200 feet high, and from the west they make quite an impression. Imagine something like the mountains on the Norwegian coast of Møre, only 2,400–3,000 feet taller.

The tallest of the peaks at the end of Valle Tartagine is Capo al Dente. It could be clearly seen from Calvi and the coast around that area and was regarded as impossible to climb. There had probably not been any serious attempt on it, and chances are that there had not been any tourists at all – not to mention mountain climbers – in these parts.

The station where we got off the train belonged to a little village, from which a road went approximately thirty miles to a forester's house at the end of Valle Tartagine.

We were heavily loaded when we started our trip, with fourteen days' worth of provisions, ropes, ice axes, sleeping bags and other camping equipment. It came to about ninety pounds per man. Backpacks were not as good back then as they are now, and I would guess that we resembled the man in the advertisement who is unfortunate not to be furnished with Bergans' ski wax.

Thirty miles in this manner did not look bright, and soon we began to look for means of transportation. After a bit of looking we found it in the form of a mule with a driver. It was not so easy to communicate with him, because this was again one of those situations that the phrasebook had not foreseen. After we in vain had tried those conversations one would normally have with delivery boys and taxi drivers – all of which were about bringing you and your luggage to either a railroad station or a hotel – we gave up on the phrasebook and resorted to sign language. Strangely enough, we finally succeeded in making the mule driver understand that we wanted the luggage brought on the mule and that the trip was to go inland. As preliminary payment we agreed on two big, fake silver coins. (It is quite possible that our fake money in reality was viable coin in Corsica – we never heard any direct protests in any case.)

As a means of transportation a mule probably has many advantages, but the means of control of a practically physical nature used to start horses or locomotives, for example, are insufficient where mules are concerned. You then have to either rely on serendipity or you must use special psychological methods. Our mule driver certainly must have known his animal from a long period of cooperation.

The mule stood patiently still while all the baggage was loaded, after which it continued to stand still. Its master started out in a light and teasing tone, first saying something like 'Hey' or 'Go', then continuing with rather coarse swear words, including derogatory slurs against its mother, father and relatives. He then beat the mule with a long stick and finally ended up spitting at it from behind. Only the latter helped, and the driver seemed to know this too; but the thing was, probably even this choice insult would not have had the right psychological effect had not the mood first been built up by the introductory exercises. When the driver had reached the spitting stage, the mule suddenly started to trot along, whereupon the driver ran after it, launched himself and jumped on to it from behind. Things were advancing nicely until the animal got tired and stopped.

The entire ceremony had to be repeated, and the forward movement of the procession was therefore in a way divided into a shock troop rush followed by the infantry that advanced steadily at an even pace. That's how it went for several miles, but then we reached the snow and the whole thing came to a halt. There wasn't much snow on the road – maybe half a foot or so to start – but both the mule and its master were convinced that it was not possible to advance in snow. Neither threats, entreaties nor promises of further rewards helped, and at last we had to unload and plod on in the snow.

As expected, it was heavy going, especially since the snow soon became deeper and it started to grow dark. We thought it best to look around for lodgings.

We soon found a little stone shed of the kind shepherds use in summer; it even had a solid roof, so that the hay and twigs on the floor were nice and dry. There are many such stone sheds across the lower mountain regions in Corsica. They are reminiscent of the simple cattle camps you find somewhat higher up than the Alpine farms in Norwegian mountain areas. When the roof is tight they are fine for spending the night. A little breezy perhaps, for even if there is sometimes a door there are never any window panes. However, one can almost always fix this with paper, pieces of board or a couple of wet jackets that must be hung up to dry anyway.

We thought we should celebrate the first evening of the real expedition with a feast. There was ample opportunity and since we would have to carry our provisions the next day, we agreed that heavy things should be used. Therefore, we had canned tuna and American corned beef to go with the hot chocolate made with a can of Nestlé cream. Certain in our conviction that we had lightened our load for the next day, we crawled into our sleeping bags and fell asleep.

The next morning we had about seven miles of deep snow to plod through before we came to the inner part of Valle Tartagine and the forester's house there.

In the past, Valle Tartagine belonged to Corsica's best-known forest districts. From this valley and other high mountain valleys, the Phoenicians, Romans and later the Genoese procured the pine needed for their boatbuilding. The forest was so dense and strong in Corsica that it was not until around 1600 that the rich Corsican forests had been completely eradicated.

Forestry then lay dormant for a few hundred years, but sometime in the middle of the nineteenth century the state began to show interest in this source of income. All land above a certain altitude was declared state property, unless proof to the contrary was provided. Foresters were brought to the valleys with the best-known forests. Around 1860, or possibly a little later, a new form of snobbery began to develop which suddenly gave the forest areas in the Corsican mountain valleys an unexpected economic allure. This was the pipe snobbery.

In one way or another a few leading companies in the pipe business found out that no finer pipes could be made than those made from the roots of a certain tree that existed only in Corsica. The briar pipe presumably took its name from a sort of French juniper called *bruyère*. It does not exist in Corsica nor is it suitable for making pipes.

Of the old, sometimes hundreds of years old, pine-tree roots, thanks to the earlier plunder there were an unlimited amount in the Corsican mountain valleys; and this kind of tree root can, just like many other kinds of roots, be used to make pipes. On this basis, the French state and some big English firms organised a nice business. While roots in normal exploitation (tar making and such) may perhaps have brought twenty francs per ton, per ton of old root one could make approximately 500 pipe blanks. With an average weight of one pound per piece, this would make approximately 1,000 pipes. These pipes were sold for prices varying from five shillings to ten pounds, and in this way the price of one ton of old root could go up to approximately 25,000 francs rather than twenty francs. It is easy to understand that with such an ample margin one might find room for a little profit here and there.

The main source of old roots was found in the upper parts of Valle Tartagine and a few tributary valleys, but the extraction took place only in summer. Those seven miles to the forester's house took us more than five hours – and we struggled hard. It is not so strange that the people of Corsica regard it as impossible to go anywhere in snow.

In the lower areas – meaning around 2,100–2,400 feet – the snow is usually completely rotten and you sink straight to the bottom. We sometimes have this type of snow in Norway, and skis are of no great help there, either. When you get higher up (and in lower temperatures), the snow gets better. But to get that far you first have to get through a few miles of slush.

The foresters proved to be a nice French family with members from three generations of both genders. We were well received; several months had passed since they had seen people from the outside (and someone like us they had probably not even seen at the cinema).

The forester himself, who belonged in the middle generation, had once worked in the areas north of Nice and was well informed about high mountains. But he also regarded the snow around there as hopeless, except quite early in the morning after a clear night. He had no knowledge of skis.

We were served coffee, fresh bread, cheese and dried meat and in return could offer Crosse & Blackwell marmalade along with some pieces of chocolate for the younger generation.

We then discussed the route up the valley. The forester told us that there was a stone shed about seven miles up, but he did not know what kind of condition it might be in. Reaching it would not be so easy either, he thought, for in many places there were several feet of snow. But if the night was clear and cold, we might be able to go early the next morning.

We decided to make an attempt and be on the trail before sunup with about half our equipment. Getting there with the full load was regarded as hopeless. When we stayed in open terrain, the snow crust held and it went well, but in those places where we broke through we were soon up to our waists. Fortunately this did not happen very often.

After a three-hour trip we came to the stone shed. It was nicely located in a little field down by the river, but it had one major disadvantage: the roof had fallen in and the shed was full of snow. No camping place.

Now we were in a fairly annoying situation. We were on the south side of the valley and there were practically no areas free of snow. The north side looked good but to get there we would have to cross the river, which was open, fast and – we had to assume – quite cold.

None of the various options available to us were particularly enticing. One possibility was to return to the forester's house, where there was a bridge across the river, but as soft as the snow had become there was little reason to believe we would get there before nightfall. We faced the same difficulty if we continued up the valley until the river got smaller and possibly covered in snow. Spending the night on the side of the river, where we found ourselves and where the ground everywhere was covered in copious amounts of soft snow, was hardly attractive, particularly when we had the north side of the valley with its many dry, nice patches over on the other side of the river. The last possibility – and the one we decided on – was to try to get across the river, at roughly where we were. This did not look to be so easy.

We could not see any places where the river was shallow enough to simply wade across, and it was sufficiently fast that it was doubtful we could escape intact to the other side should we slip in up to our chests. It was obvious that we needed to use the rope in some way, and a little above the ruined stone shed we found a suitable place where we could do just that, as the river went through a few bends. In such cases you can use the rope by fastening or holding it in the upper turn of the bend while the one who is crossing the river ties himself to the lower end of the rope, so that he gets into approximately the same situation as the weight on the free end of a pendulum. When the first man has come across or has made the turns back and forth to get oneself and the baggage over, the partners change roles so that the one who has made it over holds the rope steady, while the other swings across tied to the free end of the rope. In this way you can get across fairly fast rivers, either walking on the bottom or drifting on the surface in about the same way as the fishing gear called an 'otter trawl'. Although the technique is all right and completely safe, it is quite an awful job when the water is close to 0° Celsius.

In the name of safety, we took off all our clothes except the hobnailed boots and I made a careful trip over, first without bringing any baggage. When it proved to go well, the only thing left to do was to go back again and get the baggage across in as few trips as possible. Then it was George's turn to go back and forth a few times. Eventually we had all the equipment across and in a dry place, and we gathered everything together away from the river, on a spot free of snow on the north side.

I have never been able to understand people who like to take ice-cold baths, and I think it borders on dishonesty when someone insists that it is not very uncomfortable. But you can say one thing in its favour, as you can for all particularly uncomfortable situations: it is an exquisite pleasure when the discomfort ends, for example getting out of the cold water into the sunshine. I think it is an exaggeration to take ice-cold baths for such a reason. It reminds me too much of an idiot who bangs himself in the head with a hammer because it is nice when he stops.

We managed to light a fine fire and cooked some soup while we dried our boots and put on our clothes again. Then we had to look for a suitable camping place. The difficulty here on the north side of the river was not to find patches free of snow – there were plenty of them – but to find a more or less level one. In general the hillside was rather steep, and it was particularly the steep parts that were free of snow.

Some distance up the valley and several hundred feet above the valley floor, we finally found a suitable place. Right in the middle of a forty-five- to fifty-foot crag, we saw a big, completely horizontal platform, the innermost part of which was covered by an overhang so that a cave was formed. The platform was awkwardly located in the crag, and somewhat of a problem to reach, but in the end we solved it so that one of us stayed below the platform with all the baggage while the other went all the way to the top of the crag and lowered himself down to the platform. We could then haul up the baggage and arrange the campsite.

Further investigation of the campsite and its possibilities did not occur that evening. We gathered some pieces of wood for a fire and managed more or less to level off the worst rough spots for our sleeping bags. That night was cold and not quite comfortable: the sleeping bags were not intended for winter use. They were quite light sailcloth sleeping bags with a wool lining, and even with all our clothes on it got quite cold in the few degrees below freezing.

But the next morning in nice weather and warm sunshine, we began to get installed. The main thing was to provide water and fuel, in addition to better arranging the place where we would sleep.

There was water nearby. Some fifty to sixty feet away in the same crag a little waterfall sprayed down, and we arranged a fine access over to it; we held on to a stretched rope with the innermost hand while we had a foothold in small ledges in the mountain, and carried the bucket with the outer hand. Above the outcropping, which covered the central part of the campsite, the forest terrain continued with lots of big stumps, loose roots and tree trunks pulled down by rockslides or wind.

It was especially the big, fat pine roots that were of interest to us. The fact that these same roots were of interest to the state's forest management and to pipe manufacturers did not bother us. The roots were ideal for campfires, and once one of the big stumps was lit, the fire kept going for hours – from the evening through the night – without us having to think about it again. What does it matter under such circumstances that a few thousand kroner are spent per night?

The day was spent arranging our camp: piling stones together for a table and chairs, gathering twigs and moss for bedding under the sleeping bags and otherwise doing household chores. When evening arrived we crawled, tired and satisfied, into our sleeping bags under the rock wall, while the flames from a 3,000-kroner fire made a cosy separation between us and the cold night.

The main purpose of the trip to Valle Tartagine was to climb Capo al Dente at the end of the valley. Our camp rested at around 3,600–3,900 feet, and we had about that same distance to go to the top of the mountain.

The difficulties concerning the ascent were first and foremost that we were too lazy to get up early enough in the morning. The fact is that the most comfortable part of the night, when you spend it outdoors like this, is during the first few hours after the sun has come up and warmed the air. It is highly unpleasant to crawl out of the sleeping bag while it is still pitch dark, to cook food and then get organised to be able to start preferably a little before sunup. But it was necessary to do this in order to make it up the inclines without too much effort. When the sun had been up for two or three hours, the snow had already become soft, or the crust was no longer strong enough to carry us, and we sank in to our knees at every step.

We noticed this the first day we tried to get to Capo al Dente. It took us five or six hours to go the approximately seven miles to the foot of the mountain, and that day climbing the mountain became unthinkable. However, we were able to see the peak at close range and came to the temporary conclusion that it would serve no purpose to try it from the east or the north – the aspects we had the opportunity to study. If there were any possibility, we had to get to the pass on the south side of the peak. We plodded back down and reached our campsite at about sundown. The fire we had started in the morning was still going, so it paid to use expensive wood.

We decided to sleep late the next morning and also to use the day to fetch the rest of our equipment from the forester's house. We were hoping to get up in time the morning after that. We managed to do so, and came up to the pass on the south side of Capo al Dente after a two-and-a-half-hour, easy trip on a hard snow crust. There we sat down to study the view. The height of the peak from the pass is not particularly impressive – a few hundred feet. But on the west side, the side that faces the Mediterranean, there is a drop of 4,500–6,000 feet before you reach gentler terrain.

Far down below us we could see the coast of the Mediterranean and the little port of Calvi.

Capo al Dente belongs among those few mountains that defy climbing – in other words, a mountain in the first category. All the sides of the mountain are absolutely vertical. The peak has two tops separated by a deep gap, with the western top slightly higher than the other. At first we tried to get up some vertical gutters to the gap between the two tops, but had to abandon that. Then we had to try the south ridge of the main top, the one all the way out on the edge toward the precipice to the west. Here the difficulty was, first and foremost, that the lowest thirty to sixty feet of the ridge were overhanging and completely smooth. Right up against the overhang, however, was a little rock needle separated from the main ridge by a crevice a few feet wide, and we managed to get up on it. From the top of this needle over to the ridge on the main top the distance was not too great; George, with his long legs, could straddle it and get a foothold in a gutter that looked like it could be used for further ascent.

In this way we got past the lower part of the ridge's overhang, and even though the mountain was practically vertical the rest of the way, it was no longer what one would call particularly difficult.

Capo al Dente must be some sort of volcanic kind of rock – the mountain was full of big, deep holes everywhere that were just right for handholds and footholds. Once we had a good start, it took us only about an hour before we stood on the top. We rested and sunned ourselves, built a fine cairn and left a pipe case with notes about the ascent in it. I got that pipe case back sixteen years later, when the top was climbed for the second time. The thing was then to get back down – the eternal next question when you have reached a peak. The American author J.W. Muller has expressed this clearly in his book *First Aid to Naturers*, in which he stated that the only practicable result from climbing a mountain is to climb down again. Those who descend are known as survivors.

George and I belong to the latter category.

It is, practically speaking, always easier to get down than to get up – something most people find difficult to believe. But the situation is that when you are going down a route you have previously come up, you know first of all that it is possible to proceed, and second that you can almost always find help in the rope by placing it around a rock outcropping and then abseil down in places where it would perhaps otherwise be difficult to find any footholds. Thanks to our energy that morning, we were home early and had plenty of time to prepare a feast of a dinner to celebrate our first ascent.

Next morning it turned out that we had become victims of overwhelming laziness. From the top of Capo al Dente we had seen a series of peaks along the north side of Valle Tartagine that it would probably have been interesting to visit, but whether it was related to the reaction after the successful first ascent or the excessive enjoyment of fresh mountain air, we were in either case too lazy to do anything other than ordinary camp maintenance and a little climbing around the rocks in the neighbourhood. That's how it went the next day too, and on the morning of the third day we broke camp and went back down to the forester's house.

The plan from there was to get across to the southern mountain chains and to the village of Calacuccia on the south side of Corsica's tallest mountain, Monte Cinto. By previous agreement Calacuccia was where we were to meet Max, who had travelled there with a tent and various other items to complete the expedition's equipment.

I told George we should do something for the forester and his family. I must have had the idea that once we had penetrated into this country, we ought to do something to spread culture among the natives. In general the white race's discovery of unknown countries has only resulted in those countries' inhabitants getting venereal diseases and learning to drink alcohol. George and I now had the opportunity to rectify this reputation by making a positive cultural effort. The situation was that I had seen, in one of the forester's outbuildings, a big, old oak barrel, and in connection with the long, snowy slopes along the ridges on the south side of the valley had got it into my head to introduce the sport of skiing to Corsica.

We came down to the forester's house around dinner time. We were greeted with the customary hospitality and when, over coffee, we had told of the ascent on Capo al Dente, I continued by giving the forester and his sons a description of the sport of skiing that they unfortunately did not understand much of. But there was no objection when I asked permission to use four of the barrel staves; in the course of the evening the first Corsican ski factory was started, and the first two pairs of skis were made ready.

Barrel staves have their use as fine skis – although they are not really suitable for going uphill. The question of the bindings was solved with nails and strong string. When the whole thing was ready, the barrel-stave skis were fastened to the boots in the same way as skates. There was no possibility of moving the heel, which should not be necessary anyway. This was about the same as what have later become slalom bindings. The boots were placed on the back part of the ski and on either side of the boot fastening we nailed some short metal bands for the sake of steering. There is reason to believe that this was the first slalom ski with metal edges ever made. After a cold, clear night and a fine morning, and with the skis under our arms, we went up an open slope in the forest.

The sport of skiing has developed a lot since 1909, and bigger slalom events have certainly been held since the one we held that morning in Valle Tartagine. The audience participation has likely been greater at later events, but probably not the enthusiasm.

It turned out that the barrel stave skies were ideal for their purpose under the right snow conditions – meaning completely hard, firm snow. Steering poses no problem and the speed can be regulated by simply putting your weight back a little and braking with your rear ski – which ideally should not protrude more than half a foot beyond your boot. Instead of the two poles that are now in common use, it is practical to use a long, soft pole that you hold under the arm in the same way as the steering pole on a fishing sled. But as I said, this is on condition that the crust is strong enough to carry you even if all your weight ends up on one ski.

We noticed this on the third run. It had already become a little too mild – one ski cut through. Fortunately it was George's and he escaped without injury, except for a few scratches on his face.

After the end of the event we had an early dinner at the forester's and left the two pairs of slalom skis to his oldest sons. About the sons' fate, I have nothing to report.

By air, the distance between the forester's house in Valle Tartagine and Calacuccia is no more than approximately twenty-two miles, but you cannot use the straight line as a measure because it leads across two very high mountain chains, both over 7,500 feet: the Monte Padro and Monte Cinto chains. That would have meant a lot of plodding up and down hills in deep snow. We therefore decided to take a turn to the east in order to avoid these two mountain chains, and then into the valley that leads up to Calacuccia from a place on the east coast, a little south of Bastia.

We counted on making this trip of forty to fifty miles in about a day and a half, and started out from the forester's house in the afternoon in order to get over to the next valley south to spend the night there. However, it did not go the way we had thought, but rather just about the way we ought to have expected. The snow along the slope on the south side of Valle Tartagine was now completely soft, which meant plodding uphill with snow up to our knees. It was heavy going and slow. When we finally had come across the slope, it had already started to get dark. At the same time a mixture of snow and rain came driving in from the east. We were happy to find a stone shelter with an almost-tight roof where we could settle down for the night.

We were poorly equipped with provisions. George thought I had a lot left in my backpack, and I had thought the same about George – it turned out that we were both wrong. Our entire stock of provisions consisted of a bag of oatmeal, which we divided into two portions, one for the evening meal and one for breakfast the next morning. We hoped that we would come across an inhabited place the next day, where we could add to our provisions. In addition, the rest of our route was across such relatively low-lying terrain that we thought there was little prospect of any snow-plodding.

However, when we woke the next morning it had snowed all night and was still going. There was about a foot and a half of wet snow in front of the stone shed and farther on south the way we were going. This did not look particularly cheerful. There was no danger whatsoever, but we realised that we were looking at a few strenuous days with little prospect of food.

This annoying combination of unexpected snowfall and lack of provisions was one I experienced the following year in the Alps, also in company with George and Max. In the middle of May, we went up to a cabin – the Fridolin cabin – on the south side of Tödi, one of the highest peaks in the Glarus Alps, where we had planned to try a new route. We arrived at the cabin in nice weather and had plenty of food for three or four days, including a nice, twelve-pound beef roast.

We used the first two days to reconnoitre and to chop steps into some steep icefalls, which we had to get through to get into a place in the mountain wall that we found would give us the best opportunities.

On the third day we made a serious attempt to ascend, but had to give up because of too many rockslides. We failed to get back to the cabin in the evening, spent the night outside and came down to the cabin in good shape at dinner time the next day. By that time the beef roast had started to go quite bad and made for extremely unpleasant company in our small cabin, so we carried it carefully to a glacier some hundreds of feet away, where we sent it down a deep crevice.

We had enough food left for an evening meal and breakfast the next day, and from the cabin down into the valley it was no more than a five- or six-hour walk.

When we poked our noses out the next morning, there were three feet of new snow across the entire terrain and it was quite obvious that we could not get away for a while. We decided that the only thing to do was to make some snowshoes from the material we could find in the cabin and to try them out when the snow had settled down a little, but preferably before it began to make avalanches. The heavy new snow that falls in the Alps at that time of year usually takes three or four days to acquire the porridge-like consistency that makes it rush out in avalanches, even on relatively gentle slopes.

We ate breakfast, and that was the end of our provisions. Then we started the snowshoe fabrication and decided to make an attempt after nightfall. We had to go down a long and dangerous avalanche area and night-time was the safest. But the snow was still too loose. Even with those big snowshoes on we sank in up to our waists, and there was no question of getting anywhere. We went to bed pretty hungry and had no breakfast the following morning.

The prospect of getting away the following night was not too bright either. Around dinner time we began to talk about the beef roast. George said that maybe it hadn't been too bad after all, and Max said that in any case it certainly must be quite a bit better now after having been on ice for a few days.

Armed with ice axes and a lot of rope, we carefully plodded over to the glacier where the roast had been deposited. From the edge of the glacier crevice we could see it lying on a protuberance some forty to fifty-five feet down in the ice.

As usual, we let Max have the honour of the most uncomfortable part of the work and lowered him down to the bottom of the crevice, where he skewered the roast with the ice axe pick before we pulled him up again.

The only provision we had left was, luckily, pepper. We cut the rank-smelling roast into thin slices which were peppered thoroughly on both sides and fried in a little fat that was left. I have to say that it tasted quite strange. In some bites the pepper had the upper hand, in others the rank meat, but nobody complained.

It was not possible to get down the next night either and for another day we lived on the rank and peppered beef roast, along with endless amounts of melted snow. Around two o'clock the next morning we tried again, and now the snow had compacted enough for the snowshoes to carry us. It became an exciting trip, as right after sunup, the avalanches started. Not these quick, light-dust avalanches there are so many of in winter, but heavy, sticky, slow avalanches that came tumbling down the slopes like cement porridge.

We were walking with several hundred feet of distance between us and, as is common practice in such cases, a long, wool thread was attached to each one of us to facilitate the digging out, in case one of us should be overtaken by the porridge.

We just made it. I still remember a long run down a slight valley incline with a thick, wet, broad avalanche right at my heel. The avalanche did not move quickly, but neither was it so easy to advance quickly in the wet snow with big, clumpy snowshoes on my feet. Should you be so unlucky as to stumble in such a situation, there isn't much more to be said. That's what happened to me in the end, but fortunately I had come down sufficiently far that the avalanche stopped just as it reached me. My legs were stuck fast in the wet snow, and I had to get help from the others with ice axes to get free.

In our current situation, George and I could have taken solace in knowing it would get much worse later, but that is always rather meagre solace, and in any case we did not know it at that time.

After eating the rest of the oats, we plodded on southward, tired and hungry. There was no question of being able to reach Calacuccia. We had to come to grips with having to spend another night in the open, and only far into the next day did we reach the Calacuccia valley, where a basic road goes up past the village and across to the western part of the island. No buildings, so no prospect of getting any food before we arrived. The weather was now nice and warm, but after a while we became terribly hungry.

I remember very well how I was thinking of canned meatballs, and several times while going up the hills toward Calacuccia I saw the big cans with their familiar coloured labels in the road, a hundred feet ahead of me.

The mood had also become extremely bad, so in the name of safety we walked far apart from each other in order to avoid unnecessary quarrels. But this trip too came to an end, and on toward the afternoon the village was suddenly in front of us, just a few hundred feet away.

Vacationing in Calacuccia

During our stay in Bastia, we had been told that there were two hotels in Calacuccia, the Hotel de la Poste and the Hotel de France, the latter of which reputed to have a bathroom. We had decided on the latter.

At first we were not terribly interested in the thing about the bath. First and foremost, we were after food, and not long after our arrival we were ensconced in the inn, shovelling incredible amounts of goat meat and artichokes into ourselves. When we had eaten as much as we could in one go-around, we ate dinner once more.

Of course this was a heavier load than even the most robust digestive system could manage, and the first night as well as the subsequent twenty-four hours most of our time was spent in excursions to Hotel de la Poste, located on the other side of the street, because it turned out that the sanitation facilities were distributed between the two hotels (our hotel had the bath).

We agreed that such luxury must be exploited, and the following morning we asked that the bath be readied for use. The hotel manager had obviously not expected anything like that, and our request led to considerable confusion. They certainly had a bath, explained the manager, but it had been some time since last it was used. Besides, he was not sure where it was. After a house search, the bath finally came to light. It was a roomy zinc tub, stashed away in a basement room, filled with an incredible amount of rubbish and also an ill-tempered female cat, who had appointed a part of it into a nest for six kittens.

We were determined in our quest for cleanliness, and under George's energetic leadership the tub was relieved of its contents of old rubbish and cats and carried up to our common bedroom, where it was placed in the middle of the floor. Then we set the women to work to heat bathwater in big containers, and before dinner – which we now, informed by experience, savoured in moderation and with care – we were bathed and shaved.

That day we also had a letter from Max saying he had been somewhat delayed, so that we would have to wait for him another few days in Calacuccia. This was not such a bad idea: we needed a few days of restoration after the quick change between starvation and overeating that we had just gone through.

In the evening two new guests arrived at the hotel, two really nasty guys who drank and made noise in a way we found most objectionable. We agreed that they must be travelling salesmen, but our host later told us they were police agents out to gather information about a colony of bandits. The host didn't like them either. He was Corsican and probably related to the bandits.

From long and painful experience, I knew George's unbelievable ability to get mixed up in fights whenever the slightest opportunity arose, and I regarded the future in a dark light. My dire premonitions turned out to be right, but in a completely different way than I had expected.

Aside from a little incident the following night, nothing much happened. George and I had gone early to bed, still a little tired from our culinary experiences. A few hours into the night, George awoke and told me that he unfortunately needed to pay a visit to the other side of the street. There was nothing for it. It had become pitch dark outside and George took along one of our lamps, a rather heavy contraption. (Later on those kinds of lamps were made of aluminium and mica, but at that point we had not come that far.)

After having waited a while for George, I heard excited voices in the street outside. I had a fair idea of what that might mean and went to the window to see the details of the fight from as safe a position as possible. Just as I reached the window, I saw the lamp designate a big circle in the vertical plane and heard the crash as it splintered on the head of one of the performers. Afterwards it was completely dark, but I clearly heard the sound of another of them smashing on to the cobblestones.

A few minutes later, George came up to the bedroom. The lamp was fairly undone but looked as if it could be repaired when we paid for new glass. George had, he said, entered into a conversation with what he took to be the two inebriated, unpleasant, new hotel guests and had, to be on the safe side, immediately hit one of them in the head with the lamp. While there was still a glimmer of light, he had had time to give the fellow a kick in the groin, which was probably unpleasant, since George on this occasion was wearing his hobnail boots as slippers.

In general you could say that George in such situations worked according to the rule that Jack London expressed so poetically in the book *The Sea Wolf* and which can be summarised as such: 'When a man is down kick him in the pants, and if he gets up kick him again.'

An excellent guide for people who insist on getting into critical situations.

George did not think he would be recognised, he said. We were aware, in any case, that his alibi could be easily corroborated by my committing perjury. We then gave ourselves over to ten hours of the kind of sleep that follows when your conscience, whether good or bad, is sufficiently tired.

There was nice, warm weather the next day and after breakfast – where we stayed away from goat meat, artichokes and oil – we felt so good that we decided we would make a trip up toward Monte Cinto. We decided not to climb this sad, third-rate mountain, but to gain a little bit of an overview of the region and do a little climbing exercise on the knolls we might encounter.

We walked as far as we could without trudging through snow, and since we were moving along the southern slope we came up to a little over 6,000 feet. From there we had a fine view of the mountains around Valle Calasima, which was our next goal.

Closest to Calacuccia in the direction we would be going were the five peaks of Cinque Frati, which looked like fun, and behind them Paglia Orba, which is one of the highest peaks on Corsica (8,284 feet).

We sunbathed, ate the food we had brought along and practised climbing in the lightest possible attire. Then we sauntered on down again through the *macchia*.

We were just hungry enough to be looking forward to dinner when we got home. I was walking ahead, George thirty to forty feet behind me, and we were following some sort of cow or goat track leading in the right direction.

As I was walking along, I suddenly saw a snake lying coiled up in the middle of the trail. It was grey-black, looked to be bigger than a viper and made a menacing impression.

I stopped and signalled to George. 'It would be best if we get around this,' I said. 'This one doesn't look good.'

But it wasn't for nothing that George had grown up on a sheep farm in Australia. He stood looking at the snake with an almost sentimental interest. It was as if a little part of his fatherland had come back to him.

'Excuse me,' said George. 'Just a moment.' Then he walked toward the snake until he was about a foot away from it. The snake was calmly coiled, but with its neck stretched up and its head about five inches above the ground. I thought the whole thing looked less than nice.

George bent down slowly toward it and held his right index finger in front of it at a distance of some fifteen inches. The snake pulled back its head a little. While he moved his right index finger slightly in front of the snake, which was ready to attack, George suddenly grabbed it across the neck between thumb and index finger of his left hand and lifted it up. It was a little more than three feet long.

Now what, I thought, while in the name of safety keeping a reasonable distance. With his right hand, George took a little penknife out of his pocket, got out the smallest blade and squeezed the snake around its jaws so that it hung there with its mouth open. In much less time than it takes to describe it, he performed an elegant operation with the penknife and removed the two curved fangs from its upper jaw. I have thought ever since that George should have become a dentist rather than a professor of organic chemistry.

'So there,' he said, 'now he is just right. We have to do something with this.' The snake was still writhing quite a bit. It was probably the first time it had been to a dentist and the extraction had probably not been pain free. 'The snake has to have a name,' said George. 'He belongs to us now and shall be our mascot.'

'What shall we call him?'

We discussed the name question back and forth for some time while the snake still hung there between George's left thumb and finger. Finally we agreed on 'James', for some reason.

If George had been a real snake charmer he should have been able to make him happily follow us by whistling a suitable tune, primarily made up of quarter notes. But George was no snake charmer, and furthermore was so unmusical that even the step between whole notes was completely beyond him.

Such things mean nothing, however, for the goal-oriented. We relinquished two boot laces, tied them together and made a loop around James' neck with one end while George held the other in his hand. Then all went well until we came the outskirts of the village.

'George,' I said then, 'I think this will attract attention. Couldn't we find a less conspicuous way to bring the animal home?'

'Of course,' George answered, hauled the snake up, stuffed it in his jacket side pocket and buttoned the pocket flap. That's how we got back to the village and the hotel without attracting any kind of attention.

As we came down into the village, we had both worked up a huge thirst and sat down in the hotel's combination pub and dining room to drink sour wine mixed with water. The table in the corner was set for four; obviously someone had thought that George and I would have dinner with whatever was left of the two police agents after their conversation with George the night before. George and I did not think this was a good idea, and we agreed that we would let the others eat first and that we would bathe and change clothes before we had our meal.

We were still sitting in the pub when we heard the loud voices of our fellow guests at the entrance. They seemed to have regained their strength considerably after their night's events.

'One moment,' said George. He went over to the dining table, took the cover off a serving dish, brought James on to the table and put the cover over him.

We were in the corner once again enjoying our sour, diluted wine. When the two guests came in they appeared quite slovenly and had obviously had a strong controversy with the host, who was following them into the pub with voluble explanations. It was probably about the events of the night before. Nobody noticed us, the two quiet tourists in the other corner.

Our fellow guests immediately went to the table, one of them with his back to the wall, the other facing him with his back to the room. Between them stood the cover that hid James. They must have been very hungry. Without waiting for any additional arrivals from the kitchen one of them grabbed the serving dish, the other the cover, whereupon James – who had perhaps been bored in the dark – snaked out, in the literal sense of the phrase. This was probably not what the two dinner guests had expected. On the contrary, they expressed instantaneous surprise, almost horror. The one sitting with his back to the wall jumped up on the bench he was sitting on and ran across the table, across the floor to the exit door. The other one started to scream, threw himself backward (James had obviously aimed at him) and fell to the floor along with the chair.

Approximately fifteen seconds after James was set free, George and I were alone in the dining room.[1] As soon as the door had slammed shut behind our two friends, George went over to the table where James was carefully moving between glasses and bottles, grabbed him by the neck and stuffed him into his right-hand pocket. Then he returned to our corner and we continued our quiet thirst-quenching, though not for long.

Barely a minute went by and here came the host, the hostess, the hotel boy and girl, followed by the two frightened guests.

---

1 That I consistently refer to James in the male gender and that we also gave him a masculine name is not related to our knowing his gender. Personally I cannot tell the difference between a male and a female snake, and even George, who was somewhat of an expert, later confided that he did not know the difference either.

George and I quietly continued to drink. From all the talk and the shouting that now arose, it appeared that the two dinner guests had seen a snake on the table. The host shook his head. It was not possible. He appealed to George and me. No, we had been sitting there quietly the whole time and were very surprised at the two dinner guests' unseemly behaviour, but otherwise we had not noticed anything.

A thorough search of the room, which at any rate was so sparsely furnished that the search was very easy, quickly revealed that there was no snake there. George and I shrugged our shoulders, winked at the host who surely was familiar with delirium tremens, and went to our room to bathe and prepare for our dinner.

On the way up, George had a happy idea, went into our fellow guests' room, took James out of his pocket and placed him in one of their beds. He folded the duvet well over him and told me he was certain it would stay there. His experience with snakes in Australia had shown that they liked nothing better than being in a good bed covered by a nice duvet.

During the entire time it took George and me to bathe, dress and eat dinner, there was an agitated discussion going on between the host and the hotel staff and the two unwanted guests. The host, who among other things had his hotel's reputation to consider, managed to pacify them by pouring them large quantities of a horrible kind of Corsican spirit, made from figs imported from Sardinia.

George and I had gone to bed when the two of them finally came tottering up the stairs and staggered into their room right next to ours. It was quite interesting to follow the events in the other room from the sounds that penetrated into ours. We heard them take off their boots, then one or the other staggered into a chair, probably to hang up a jacket and trousers, and finally we understood that they were ready to go to bed in the dirty shirts and wool underpants they wore every day.

And then the fun started again. I will not deny the possibility of there being animal lovers for whom going to bed inebriated with a snake represents the epitome of cosiness, but even if this should be the case, our neighbours certainly did not belong to this non-prejudicial type. I do not think I have ever experienced so wild a scream as the one we heard that time exactly at the moment we had expected. Then we heard the sound of bare feet going past our door and down the stairs, accompanied by excited shouts and speech.

'Just a moment,' said George. He slipped out of bed, and put on his jacket. Thirty seconds later he was back in our room and put the jacket on the back of the chair next to his bed. He had found James in the middle of the floor and now he was in his jacket pocket, to which by now he must have become accustomed. James was behaving quite calmly.

Then followed the same story involving the entire hotel staff coming up to the room of our two fellow guests and thoroughly scouring the room with excited talk and shouts. But there was no James. The host also knocked on our door and received a heap of complaints from us about these hotel guests who made noise and disturbed peaceful people's sleep. We then stayed quietly in our beds listening to the others pack up their things and move to Hotel de la Poste.

This was also in reality the most reasonable, since the bath – which was Hotel de France's big attraction – had been appropriated by George and me.

Max arrived the next day. He brought tent equipment and new provisions and was full of energy. The following morning we bid a fond farewell to our host, who received James as a gift. I am not sure he kept him for long. He did not seem to be able to give James his due for services rendered.

The expedition to the mountains around Valle Calasima

We had agreed to move the expedition's base camp to the innermost part of Valle Calasima, a mountain valley stretching in a direction approximately north–south, not far from the west coast of Corsica.

As already mentioned regarding mountain formations in general, Corsica has the same peculiarities as Norway, meaning the foothills and mountains begin very gradually from the east and end with the biggest and steepest peaks all the way toward the narrow fjords on the west coast.

To get from Calacuccia to Valle Calasima we first had to follow the road westward for a bit and then take a mule track in a northerly direction. We managed to obtain a mule and its owner and loaded the tent and as much as possible of the other baggage on to the animal. We set out with enough provisions for a couple of weeks.

By the low end of Valle Calasima there is a little village, from which the valley takes its name – or perhaps it has taken its name from the valley – and this was the last inhabited area before we entered the mountain regions. These little Corsican mountain villages have probably changed very little in the last couple of thousand years. They consist of one or two narrow streets with houses made of clay and stone stuck together, and every once in a while you see the remains of some fortification on a rise in the middle of the village.

At the time when we visited Corsica, the villages were ruled by a priest and/or a bandit – often both. (God knows if the priest didn't also sometimes take a bandit job as additional employment.) The village of Calasima belonged to the peaceful kind of village. The bandit villages and the bandit areas in general are mainly somewhat farther south in the region around one of Corsica's highest peaks, Monte Rotondo.

It is not possible to know how we would have been received had we arrived unaccompanied in Calasima. In all probability we would have been treated with the utmost degree of suspicion. This village could not have been visited by strangers very often.

As we would have liked to buy some goat meat to take along, we started negotiating with the priest. He spoke a kind of French, and as the village chief he quickly organised our supplies. But there were other things that interested him more: we had told him that we were students from Switzerland, something that convinced him we must certainly have knowledge of medicine. He was of the opinion that the current incidents of sickness in his village were something we should take care of and conquer *en passant*.

It did not help us to protest. We had to do what we could. There was one old woman in particular that the priest thought there was little hope for – and that was how she looked, too.

Few people, if any, in southern Europe at that time had less of an idea of the science of medicine than George, Max and I, and our medical kit was very sparsely equipped. We agreed that the old lady probably was experiencing the last stages of tuberculosis. Judging from her appearance, she might be suffering from any and all deadly diseases.

The expedition's medical equipment consisted of a small so-called travel pharmacy, no bigger than could fit in a jacket pocket. A search through the contents showed us that in terms of medicines we had only one for external use (tincture of iodine) and one for internal use (Sagrada laxative pills). We therefore had no choice, so to speak; we transferred a reasonable number of pills into a little paper cone and gave it to the priest with instructions to give the patient two pills three times a day. We thought this could not be too harmful. To be on the safe side we decided to sneak around the village on our return trip.

Accompanied by the priest's blessings and with lively, loud encouragement from the village male youths, who admired us because of our ice axes, we started into the valley.

Valle Calasima is a flat-bottomed valley and closely resembles mountain valleys in Norway. Like all such valleys in Corsica, it is not populated and is visited only in summer, because no real Corsican believes in the possibility of travelling in snow.

All the way at the end of the valley, Paglia Orba looms with its impressive vertical precipices with snow-and-ice-covered out-croppings below. On the right side of the valley we had five pointed peaks, Cinque Frati (The Five Brothers), and through a rift at about 4,500–5,000 feet to one side of Paglia Orba we could catch a view of the peaks farther out toward the coast. Among them was the famous Tafonatu, which was our first goal.

We were lucky in finding a campsite. The valley floor was flat with large snow-free patches. The little river at the bottom of the valley was free of ice and snow, and we set up the tent in a meadow close to it, right up under the foot of Paglia Orba. The meadow where we had pitched our tent was covered in rocks, moss and a juniper-like bushy growth called *macchia*, which formed dense patches across the valley floor.

The *macchia* bushes were very practical. When we came home in the afternoon or toward evening, thoroughly wet from sliding down fields of snow or hiking through slush, we had only to set a match to them to get a huge fire. This lasted for about an hour and the distance between the different patches of bush was generally big enough for the fire not to spread significantly. Among the provisions we had brought along from the village of Calasima there was some fresh goat meat that tasted lovely when cooked over the embers of the *macchia* fire.

Our first venture was to the Tafonatu mountain, which is located all the way out toward one of the narrow, steep west-coast valleys. The top of the mountain is about 7,500 feet above sea level, and the mountain is in the shape of a huge plate of slate stood on end, with a serrated top ridge and impressive, practically vertical precipices on both sides. Several hundred feet under the top ridge there is a hole through the mountain and even that far down the mountain is no more than sixty to ninety feet wide.

As we know, there are several of these mountains with holes.

In the Alps you have Gross Tschingelhorn and in Norway there is Torghatten with its hole formed by Vågekallen. Geologists have different theories about how these holes were formed, but they are probably not correct. The only theory that seems to have any kind of reason to it, and which is heard in Corsica about Tafonatu and in Switzerland about Gross Tschingelhorn, is that the holes were formed a considerable time ago during a feud between the archangel Gabriel and the Devil.[1] One of these gentlemen was hunted by the other, who pursued him with weapons; in some tales there is talk of throwing hammers and, in others, boulders. In critical situations the pursued one – whether the Devil or the archangel – placed suitably big stone plates in front of himself as a shield and, naturally, these remain standing in the holy state in which one now finds them.

In order to reach the foot of Tafonatu, we first had to cross the rift on the south-west side of Paglia Orba, a tiring ascent of about 2,100–2,400 feet, most of it in deep, soft snow. On the last part of the glacier toward the rift the snow was good and firm, but the climb was very steep. We ended up under a snow overhang that we had to chop and dig a tunnel through to get into the rift. Then it was an easy trip along the mountainside on Paglia Orba's south-west side over to the rift between Paglia Orba and Tafonatu.

It is steep from the rift up to the long top ridge of Tafonatu, but here, as well as in many other places in the Corsican mountains, there are lots of handholds and vertical walls that look hopeless from a distance but often do not pose bigger problems than climbing the ladder wall in a gym.

After an hour and a half of fun climbing we stood on Tafonatu's highest peak. Its ridge, which stretches southward, is what in mountaineering terms is called 'exposed'. A deep rift separated us from the nearest peak, which stuck up into the sky like a long, black finger, and was etched sharply against the snow-white

---

1 The version that has the feud taking place between the Devil and Saint Martin has less to recommend it. Even one who is not a geologist will have the distinct impression that the holes must date from a much earlier period.

mountains and the Mediterranean glittering in the background. The sharp and serrated ridge with an often-overhanging rim stretched from the bottom of the rift to the top and showed us the way. There was no danger of taking the wrong path.

We realised this as soon as we glanced down the slippery, vertical mountainsides toward the east and west. We would have to keep to the ridge, and that is what we did.

Traversing Tafonatu's two peaks is an airy trip. It's a matter of keeping your tongue straight in your mouth and not swaying from side to side. But as I said, the path is self-evident.

General opinion seems to hold that once you've told the story of how you got to the top of a mountain, you should continue and describe the view. I've never been able to agree. A view may possibly be nice to look at, and a painter or photographer can often make much of it to the later benefit of others, but stories about the view are in my opinion generally some of the saddest to appear in literature.

Weather, or rather bad weather, can be exploited in literature because bad weather has a dynamic character and may entail events of different sorts, something we know from different authors such as Henrik Wergeland and Rex Beach. This is practically never the case so far as views are concerned, although our view from the top of Tafonatu was an exception – meaning the view forty-five degrees down toward the west. Here Tafonatu forms a vertical wall that closes a mountain valley, Valle Nebbio (Fog Valley), as it was called on the map. While we were climbing across the Tafonatu Ridge, the fog cover was spreading across the valley and we could see down to a field that we thought was maybe 3,000–4,500 feet below.

This field was evidently inhabited. We could see something resembling a village down there, and through the binoculars we could also see animals or people moving about. It was quite strange because it is rare that you see permanent habitation – not to mention villages – in Corsica above the lower reaches of winter snow. This village was certainly situated at about 3,600 feet above sea level. There was practically no forest. Beyond the village the valley narrowed down again between high, vertical mountains, and from where we were standing it looked completely cut off from the outside world.

We continued along the ridge, and the next time we looked down toward Valle Nebbio, it was covered by light, white clouds.[2] On the other side of the southern peak the ridge sloped down evenly, and after a few hours of enjoyable climbing we stood on the rim of Tafonatu's narrow southern wall. This led down to a broader back that was only about 150 feet high. But it was decidedly an overhang unsuited to climbing exercises.[3]

Nonetheless, these 150 feet had to be conquered. We knew that from the rim below we could get down toward the east and reasonably go along shelves in the east wall of the mountain toward the infamous hole. The point where we were standing hung out toward the south, as I mentioned, while the east wall was in any case no more than vertical and looked to have a shelf in many places. That way we could get down to the broader back and a continuation of the ridge.

The ropes were readied, an *Abseilschlinge* was used as a secure anchor, and soon I was dangling down the worn, smooth mountainside, accompanied by wishes for a good trip from above. I landed safely on one of the shelves and found the conditions favourable for further lowering of the rope.

Contrary to our expectations, there had probably been people here before. An iron spike with a ring attached showed us we were not the first to dangle there.

The second and third man followed in a double rope which was stuck through the *Abseilschlinge* above and which was later easily pulled down after us. The same operation was repeated twice and once again we were on firm ground.

From then on it was an easy trip. A convenient shelf led us to the hole, which was photographed and admired. The floor of the

2 In *Jahrbuch des Österreichischen Alpensclubs* (*The Annals of the Austrian Alpine Club*) of 1907, Dr Gerngross talks about Valle Nebbio, which he saw from the Tafonatu Ridge. It was as usual filled with dense fog.

3 This was before the time of pitons.

hole was shaped like a big bowl that sloped slightly toward the west and ended in a steep precipice. Above the bowl was a vault of walls and roof. We estimated its height to be about thirty feet. The width of the hole was about 150 feet. The further descent was reasonably easy and we quickly came to our old route we'd followed up Tafonatu.

By sunset we reached our tent, where we were soon occupied with domestic chores. Wet boots, pants, shirts and more hung on branches stuck in the ground a suitable distance from a flaming *macchia* fire, and we danced around the fire in Roman bath getups while we each cooked a bit of goat meat skewered on long sharp sticks.

We had been in continuous motion for fifteen hours that day and we spent the next day being lazy, resting and making further plans.

The village in Valle Nebbio

George was on his stomach studying the map. 'Listen here,' he said, 'that village in Valle Nebbio doesn't exist. The valley exists but no village – not even a shelter is marked.'

That was correct. No village on the map. I thought this was quite strange. Although the map was poor as far as the high mountain areas were concerned, all the inhabited places to which there was any kind of road – even if it was only simple forester housing – we had so far been able to find on the map. George and Max, who came from Australia, thought it perfectly reasonable that also on the map of Corsica there would be blank spots, albeit small ones. The result of all this was that we decided to investigate more closely the next day and, if possible, try to find a way down there from one of the rifts on the side of Tafonatu.

It turned out to be a difficult job. From the rift between Tafonatu and Paglia Orba, passage was completely hopeless: there was only slippery, wet, almost vertical rock, 1,000 feet down. Some 1,500–1,800 feet below us the fog was dense and white, obstructing all further observation. The other side did not look any better.

We walked back down a little then and climbed up to the hole in the mountain wall. The bottom of this hole sloped evenly out toward the valley, or rather toward the precipice that formed the back wall of the valley. We walked carefully to the edge of the precipice and there we finally saw a possibility. All the way in the left-hand corner the sloping rock we were standing on continued in a kind of gutter or shelf, and it looked for the moment to provide a useable path. It was narrow and quite steep but not so bad it couldn't be walked without any real climbing.

We continued carefully down for about an hour until we reached the top edge of the fog. After that we placed properly spaced small cairns in order to be able to find our way back. The terrain became less steep after a while.

Then we noticed that there had been people here before us. Although there wasn't really any trail, here and there on the rocks and in the gravel there were clear signs of passage. In and of itself this was not so strange, for in these mountain areas there are wild Corsican sheep called *mouflon*, which are sought-after hunting prey.

Our happiness ended abruptly when we realised we were standing on the edge of an overhang that looked as if it stretched far out to each side. How far down from here we couldn't tell. The fog was thick and we could detect no bottom. So, we sat down on the edge of the precipice and ate sandwiches and smoked cigarettes. Such things happen in the mountains.

It happened once to some people who, tired and worn out, climbed down the long north side of Dents du Midi in Switzerland at dusk in fog and rain. (In fair weather there are easier ways to get down, but they kept to the ridge so as not to take the wrong path.) They ended up at a vertical cliff, and there was nothing to be seen – just fog, darkness and rain. They were wet, tired and hungry, but it was impossible to continue. As reluctant as they might be, they had to spend the night on the ridge. They found a flat place slightly back from where they had stopped, sat there the better part of the night and shivered until they fell asleep toward morning. It was already light when they were awakened by people from a cabin situated a few hundred feet away. The ridge where they had spent the night was only a few feet above flat ground.

We were much better off but had begun to come to terms with retreat when a little breath of air gave us the needed glimpse of the terrain down below. The overhang we were sitting on was no more than twenty to thirty feet high, and under it was a ladder. We saw this in one quick glimpse then everything disappeared again. But we had decided.

We pounded the ice axe securely in a fissure, fastened the rope and let ourselves down. As far as the ladder was concerned, it looked rickety and we found it safest to let the rope remain hanging there. On down through the fog we went, along something that now without a doubt could be called a trail. I think we must have gone down about 2,400 feet by the time we were under the fog layer, which meant it was approximately 1,200 feet thick. And now we saw the field with the little village right by – only a scree the size of a real ski jump separated us from it.

There were only about twenty to thirty houses, most of them quite small, but unlike the other village houses we had seen most of them were smooth and whitewashed. It later turned out that they were constructed of dried or fired bricks and coated on the outside with a kind of stucco. Aside from the buildings now in use, there were also the ruins of a few buildings that had obviously been considerably bigger.

We were used to being looked at with deep mistrust when we arrived from the mountains down into unknown villages. Considering the way we had come to look after a while, this was perhaps not so strange. The people were possibly somewhat familiar with bandits, but we undoubtedly represented a new and terrible kind. However, the attitude in this village seemed to be somewhat different from that of the various other villages where we had instilled fear on our journey. The inhabitants did look curious but in no way did they give the impression of being frightened. A group of twenty to thirty men of different ages gathered outside the village with a considerable number of women behind them. They adopted an attitude of expectation, and we did not have the impression that it was simply friendly.

We began as usual with peaceful and friendly overtures which obviously made no impression. Then George, true to form, switched to using the phrasebook. The main problem with such phrase-books is that you often are in situations that the phrasebook author had not anticipated. At such moments it is important to hit on a choice selection of comments geared toward use in some-what similar situations. George decided on a combination of the chapters 'To Make a Visit: *Far una visita*' and then the one that starts with '*Come stà?* (How are you?)'. In quick succession he read '*E a casa il Signore?* (Is the man of the house at home?)', '*Il Signore è uno straniero* (The man is a stranger)' – this one with hand gestures toward Max and me – '*La Signorina mi è molto simpatico* (This miss seems very nice to me)' and '*Viene qui angelo mio* (Come here my angel)'. These are all comments meant to create a friendly and cordial mood but when the responses predicted in the phrasebook fail to materialise, the friendly party spirit cannot be developed.

The comments George had made about the women were nevertheless not unwarranted. Although they stayed in the background a little, we could see with a swift survey that they were more beautiful than many other women in Corsica.

During George's futile work to introduce conversation with the help of the phrasebook, the men had formed a half-circle, and even for someone not particularly schooled in military strategy it was clear that what they were trying to arrive at was an encircling movement. After a while this situation started to get a little embarrassing. The old method of bringing out cigarettes, lighting them yourself and offering them to the locals had no effect whatsoever, and we increasingly had the impression that we had ended up in company where we were not welcome and should preferably not have presented ourselves.

We had already started to discuss the possibility of a hasty retreat when a new woman came out from the village and addressed the encircling male troops in a language we did not understand even one word of, but in a tone that clearly showed she was used to commanding.

At first, this did not seem to improve our situation very much; there was no longer any possibility of retreat and under the leadership of this newly arrived woman the troops, without any resistance from us, drove us into the village. The procession stopped in front of a house considerably bigger and nobler than the others, and we were requested to step inside. At this moment we had become more or less fatalistically disposed and decided to let things run their course without getting actively involved in the development of events.

Our main impression was that we had accidentally ended up in a bandit colony, and that we would probably be kept there for a while until it was discovered whether or not there was any possibility of a ransom or some such. But here we were on the wrong track. The house we had entered had a large, nice living room with a fireplace, from which doors opened into other rooms. We were shown through one of the doors and came into a bedroom where an old – some might say elderly – lady with white hair was propped up in a large bed surrounded by three or four young women. To our great surprise and also considerable relief she addressed us in a French that was, if not perfect, at least serviceable and comprehensible. In addition she was in possession of a considerable amount of the so-called French *savoir vivre*.

'Gentlemen,' she said, 'it pleases me that you have wanted to pay me a visit. As I do not have the pleasure of knowing you, perhaps you would be so kind as to tell me who you are, where you come from and what the purpose of your visit is.'

It is quite amusing to note that here she used practically the same questions that world developments during the last generation have made it necessary for anyone to answer, whenever someone arrives somewhere or other, it doesn't matter where. I can well remember the strict rules about such things, among others, at the mountain resort hotels in Norway in 1917–18, where everyone who arrived had to not only give their name, age, place of birth, where they came from and where they were going, but also the purpose of their stay. It so happens that the purpose of a stay at a high mountain resort in the middle of the most hectic season may be of various kinds, and one of my friends who came from Finse at Easter vacation protested at length by saying that this did not concern anyone else when faced with this question. It did not help in the least – he was ordered to fill out the appropriate space. He looked gravely at the chief receptionist. 'Do you really mean I must write down the true purpose?' he asked.

'Absolutely,' answered the receptionist.

He then filled out the space with a four-letter word. The chief receptionist looked at him in horror.

'No – seriously – it is not possible to write that in our registry book.'

'Well, well,' said the man, 'that's what I thought, but it is, after all is said and done, the real purpose.'

'Yes,' said the chief receptionist, 'but it won't do. We cannot allow it. You must write something else.'

My friend thought for a moment and changed the word to 'bunnyhunt'. Thereby the case was closed.

Our situation was not the same as that of my friend at Finse, and we had the embarrassing impression that whatever we now might say would play quite a big part in our future. We stuck to the truth, said that we had come from Switzerland where we were studying and that we had come through Italy to Corsica to climb mountains. I described Norway a little. George and Max said a bit about Australia. It made about as much of an impression as Marco Polo's descriptions at the time made on the Venetians. Nevertheless, the old lady did not seem to be particularly nasty-minded. On the contrary, she regarded us with kindness and interrogated us about who else we had met in Corsica and about how we had come to have the idea of going through the hole in Tafonatu down into her valley. She said that in her lifetime and in that of her parents, it had never happened that strange people had come down into this village. What was obviously the most important to her was to uncover whether or not we belonged to some sort of government agency or other. We must have managed to convince her that this was not the case.

After some time had passed we had the distinct impression that a somewhat cordial relationship had been established. This developed in a positive direction when it turned out that the old lady smoked cigarettes – meaning she was now delighted to be lighting up one of George's Virginias.

'Now you know,' said George, 'who we are, but we have to admit we are fairly curious. Would you now tell us a little bit about yourself?'

She looked at us at length with wise old eyes and finally said, 'Yes, why not … '

With her mother and father she had come down to this village as quite a young child. Her father belonged to the well-known bandit family Bellacoscia and had, some sixty to seventy years ago, been driven north from his territory around Monte Rotondo, at which point by sheer coincidence with his wife and daughter he had come down into this valley. It was then already populated, according to our hostess, by some remnants of the communist Giovannali family, which had been practically exterminated a few hundred years beforehand.[1] At the time of our hostess' arrival in this Nebbio village, it was already primarily inhabited by women, as the men, in accordance with good old Corsican custom, killed each other as a result of private disagreements.

In the course of a short time our hostess' parents had won a position as leaders of the village; when her father some years later did not come back from one of his trips through the Tafonatu hole, her mother took over the leadership. Little by little mother and daughter instituted a purely matriarchal rule, which was so much easier because at that time there were four women to every man. To keep the stock of men at a level sufficient for the families' reproduction and to conduct the roughest labour, the remaining men were deprived of their weapons and were thereafter used in a reasonable way. But there were, she said, certain difficulties in retaining the once established relationship between men and women inasmuch as the men – when no longer allowed to shoot at one another – in the course of a certain period would arrive at approximately the same number of women and then might think of taking over the power. This was fixed in a simple and practical way, meaning that only every fourth male child was allowed to continue living. The other three were killed right after birth. You cannot say this woman was anything but efficient.

There can hardly be any doubt that the draconian manner in which the village of Nebbio was governed must have been related

---

1 Although it is not unthinkable that there may have been remnants of the Giovannali family in this valley around the year 1850, it is obvious that the original population dates from much further back. As I will later show, this must be a matter of old Greek or Phoenician colonies.

to the influence wielded by the remnants of the communist Giovannali family. That the original population of Nebbio dated from a far earlier point in time is beyond any doubt as well.

We were invited to dine with what I, for the sake of brevity, will call the mayoress, and we were given an excellent dinner. For here we met, for the first time during our stay in Corsica, the real *mouflon*, about the only domestic animal in the village.

It is well known that *mouflon* exist in Corsica, but it is very rare to encounter them. I have heard about a series of hunting expeditions for *mouflon* where the hunter never actually saw such an animal and had to content himself with shooting a tame goat. Here in Nebbio the place seethed with *mouflon* and our hostess said that according to an old tradition – which dated from a long time before her time – *mouflon* were regarded as a sacred animal, although not so holy it couldn't be milked, shorn and eaten. An old ram was the object of particular worship. It lived by itself in a small chapel or temple, and it seemed as if it was being treated just about like the Apis bull in its time.

The word *mouflon* was unknown in the village. There could be no doubt that it was the same animal that otherwise existed in a wild state only in Corsica and in Sardinia, but in the Nebbio valley it was known as *Molekki*.[2]

Gigot de mouflon, simmered in *mouflon* cream, is a dish that would certainly have caused a sensation in any gourmet restaurant in Europe in its day. We complimented the mayoress on the food – something she clearly appreciated – and then she told us her view of the animal husbandry of her village. 'We could, perhaps,' she said, 'get other animals, keep goats or even cattle, but why would we want that? Sheep have everything you need. From them

---

2 This story, which at the time when we heard it appeared quite fantastic, is in complete accordance with the results we later arrived at, namely that the original Nebbio inhabitants belonged to the Phoenician colonists from the time of 600 years before the birth of Christ. The Phoenician god Moloch, as we know, was depicted as a ram or a man with a ram's head. It obviously cannot be disregarded that at a later point in time there may have been an influx of Greek colonists. George, who had a halfway classical education, later said he recognised Greek words being used there. See *Revue Bleu*, Louis Villat's article 'Une colonie grecque en territoire française: Le village de Cargèse (Corse)', 517.

we have milk, cheese and meat, wool for clothes, leather for footwear and fertiliser. Anything more we do not need.'

And of course that is correct. If you have to get along with one animal, it has to be sheep. Practically the only thing it cannot give is eggs – but that is no loss if you do not know about it.

After the roasted *mouflon*, we were served something strongly reminiscent of macaroni, only better. The mayoress said it was the marrow of a plant that grew wild in the valley, which they had an unlimited amount of. It was called 'Fan Tan'.[3]

After a fine meal we continued our conversation with our hostess. It cannot be denied that we were a little curious about what she saw as our future. We did have the distinct impression that a visit by strangers in and of itself was not regarded with any particular kindness in the Nebbio village, and I won't say anything against that. They were obviously doing all right and preferred living by themselves. We explained that we had planned to go back to Switzerland – where we'd come from – as soon as possible, and we showed her on the map approximately which way we had travelled. Explaining to her the location of Norway and Australia was obviously not possible, but our fear of not being regarded and treated as welcome guests proved to be completely unfounded – it was rather the contrary.

---

3   We did not especially notice this dish then, other than that it tasted great. Later I have put its case to both language researchers and botanists alike and have brought to light that the word 'Fan Tan', which in Italy is used to describe a certain type of macaroni (*fanta*), is really a Tibetan word which means 'a place to eat' and which is also used about the food that is eaten in a place to eat. The Fan Tan plant still exists in the border region between China and Tibet as a species of Cycas, or a cross between Cycas and Phoenician farinifera.

As the Fan Tan plant must have come to the Nebbio valley with the original Phoenician colonisers considerably before the birth of Christ, it is obvious that the generally accepted theory about macaroni coming to Europe for the first time with Marco Polo does not hold.

It must have come some 1,500 years earlier to the Phoenicians from the Persians across Mesopotamia. The designation 'macaroni' (originally marco rondi) therefore has no real justification; it should be replaced by the more rarely used *fanta* (Fan Tan). In the name of thoroughness, the hypothesis that C.K. Chesterton presents in his article 'Scottish Influence on the Development of Latin European Languages' should be mentioned. Chesterton claims the designation 'macaroni' is purely Scottish (McAroni), but then Chesterton has, as we know, never gained any recognition as a research historian, and his above-mentioned hypothesis must probably, in the light of the knowledge of our time, be regarded as a result of a rather lively imagination. That the Fan Tan plant is no longer cultivated in Europe is probably related to the fact that one has tried to cultivate this distinctly high-mountain growth in low-lying areas.

'Since you've managed to get here,' said the mayoress as she toasted us with a glass of *mouflon* milk, 'I don't think you should be in a terrible hurry to leave.

'I tell you,' she continued, 'it isn't every day you come to a place as nice as this. Here you get good food and kind treatment – and if you'd like a little flirt, I have plenty of pretty young girls who could really benefit from a bit of change.'

'Hear, hear!' cried Max.

It cannot be denied that they sometimes find the choice of suitors they have at their disposal a bit monotonous. Of course this gave us something to think about. Two things spoke in favour of accepting the invitation. One was that the mayoress was undeniably right about the place being nice and the girls pretty. We had very quickly arrived at this conclusion, which we had already known long ago in connection with the Greek–Phoenician colony Cargèse (described by Louis Villat in *Revue Bleu*). Had we followed literature better we would have known that Louis Roule on 25 September 1900 had written an article in *Journal des Débats* entitled 'Promenade d'été en Corse', wherein he describes Cargèse women in words that cannot be misunderstood. I find I must quote some of his descriptions in the original language. We can certainly agree that the translation of the picture he paints pales in comparison: We can certainly agree that the translation of the picture he paints pales in comparison:

'Avec leur allure souple, leur taille svelte, leurs petites têtes aux grands yeux noirs, elles évoquent des souvenirs de la Grèce et elles augmentent de leur grâce aisée l'impression riante donnée par la ville et la mer.'

In our more prosaic English:

'With their supple allure, their trim figures, their small heads with big, black eyes, they evoke memories of Greece and they augment by their easy grace the pleasant impression given by the city and the sea.'

As anyone might well understand, one could here be led into temptation.

The other thing was that, in spite of the mayoress' thoroughly kind tone, we had the impression that it would be regarded as tactless should we retreat too soon. The way the situation had developed, we were to a high degree dependent on a good relationship with the old lady.

Any second thoughts among the members of our expedition came down to George's, who at that time had reason to believe he was engaged to be married. This later turned out not to have been the case, but you can never be too careful. I myself was at that time not restrained by any such scruples, but I should have been: the Christmas before I had been in Grindelwald on a sleighing trip with a girl from Brazil who was at boarding school with my sister. I had not paid any particular attention to this event, but after my return from Corsica, I received a letter from her in which she ended our engagement for the comical reason that her parents were against it. It was like hearing the signal 'DANGER OVER' without having first heard the alarm.

It wasn't so difficult to surmount George's second thoughts. A little hint from Max, to the effect that it looked like a lack of confidence in his own strength of character, was enough for George to decide that it should be subjected to the strongest possible attempts. In short, we accepted the invitation and spent a few nice days in the colony. The situation was practically the same as at any fancy high mountain resort, except for music and dance. But otherwise everything you could wish for – even card games.

The mayoress turned out to be in possession of an ancient deck of cards (God only knows how it had found its way there, but it could not possibly have been less than sixty years old). She taught us a game with thirty-two cards where the cards followed a completely different sequence from what we were used to in the game of whist.[4]

---

4 I have later discovered that it must have been the ancient French game *Trente-deux*, which Ely Culbertson discovered around 1930 and launched under the name *Jo-Jotte*.

We also had ample opportunity to become more knowledge-able about the village's different institutions, among them the chapel, or rather the combination chapel and communal slaughter-house, as it turned out to be. It was a whitewashed building with a strange wedge-shaped door opening, and above it was an inset relief with a depiction of something like a ram. In the rear of the long room was a stone statue, also of a ram, which I was later able to take a picture of. Just in front of this piece of sculpture was a stone plate of the kind that is used to put salt on for goats at high mountain shelters in Norway.

The part of worship we were able to observe had 100 per cent material aspect in that it only consisted of slaughtering a small number of selected *mouflon*, which brought on thoughts of the next day's dinner. But it is of course possible that the religion of the people of Nebbio also included other rituals than those we experienced, but if it didn't, one has to say it was simple and straightforward.

Generally speaking, I think I must confess that the period of time we came to spend, quite apart from all our plans, as guests of the mayoress in the Nebbio colony belongs among the nicest, albeit perhaps not the most nerve-tingling, chapters of our Easter vacation.

In such situations it is important, above all, to be adaptable. It is probably an inherent ability in most people but one that is most often stifled by the scruples and prejudice children are burdened with during their upbringing at home and at school. This damaging influence is something you must get rid of before it is too late, and this is not always such a simple problem. The most fortunate in this regard are those young people who early on are left on their own, for example during study abroad. It is incredible how quickly they develop a practically scruple-free mentality. Certainly this was so in the case of George, Max and me.

Late one afternoon after we had lived in the village for a few days, George approached me. 'You know,' he said, 'I think it would be good if we withdrew from this. Otherwise we'll sink into lassitude and well-being and end up as resident shepherds. That wasn't really the reason we went on a voyage of discovery.'

I thought there was something to this kind of thinking and we agreed to sneak away the next morning before daylight. In the pitch dark, about four in the morning, we met in front of the chapel. George was not the type whose instincts are spoiled by *mouflon* milk and beautiful women. 'We'll take this plaque above the door with us as a souvenir,' he said. No sooner said than done – four or five taps with the point of the ice axe around the relief[5] of the ram loosened it. It was heavy, so we put it in Max's bird bag and then we were off.

The first hour was slow going. Dawn had just begun to break and the trail we were following was not easy to see. After a while the light became better and at about six-thirty we were above the fog layer (which was lower now than when we came) and up under the overhang where we had left the rope. The rope was gone and the ladder too. Clearly our kind hosts had intended to make certain of our company until further notice.

Our escapades no longer felt like so much fun, and it would be a fairly embarrassing story should we be overtaken here and brought back down to the village. Besides, we could not be quite sure that this business with the holy ram would be regarded with much kindness. We had to find a way up, preferably within an hour or so.

The trail we had come was on a quite broad and not particularly steep ridge that narrowed after a while before it ended up against the overhang. It was about thirty feet high and completely without cracks or handholds of any kind. Straight up was impossible. Towards the south the overhang rose higher and higher from what we could see and, in any case, should we try this route we would have to go back down again quite some distance – something we for good reason had no taste for. On the north side, to the left of us, prospects looked even worse. Nevertheless, it was that possibility we had to try.

---

5   George later gave this relief of an undoubtedly old Phoenician origin to the British Museum, where it now resides. The only thing left of it in my possession is the photograph I took in very poor light while it was still in place.

The ridge we were standing on had an absolutely plumb straight north wall that ran in toward the overhang. This north face, along with the continuation of the overhang, formed a chasm that continued down until shrouded in fog. How deep it may have been I cannot say. It took about fifteen seconds before we could hear the sound from the rocks we threw down, but this is not a precise or certain method of measurement.

Things were off to a bad start. It was quite clear that we could not go even three feet beyond the edge of the chasm. However, some twelve to fifteen feet farther on there seemed to be a deep fissure in the mountain, and it even looked as if it went clear to the top of the wall where the overhang culminated. It ended in the wall of the chasm some thirty feet below us.

We decided to use Max as an offering to experiment. Thank God we had enough rope left. Max was lowered down all the way into the inner corner of the chasm until he was at about the level of the lower part of the fissure. He had neither hand nor foothold and it must have been quite uncomfortable. Then it was a question of gaining enough sideways friction between his rubber soles and the rock wall so that he could swing himself across the twelve or so feet that separated him from the fissure. It didn't work. We then lowered an ice axe down to him. Max kicked off with his right leg into the corner and managed to get the tip of the ice axe into the fissure. Soon he had hauled himself in and disappeared, but from the look of the rope we could see that he was steadily working his way up. We were not sorry to finally hear his triumphant shouts from the top, and it was not many minutes before we had the rope back in the original place.

Around twelve o'clock we were sitting in the Tafonatu hole casting a final glance over Valle Nebbio, which once again was completely covered by fog. And with his powerful, if not felicitous, voice, George sang his farewell song:

I loved a lass and her name was Lill
But she was seduced by Buffalo Bill
And then she was kissed by Seladon Hill
God damn her soul, I love her still.

In George's otherwise simple and uncomplicated nature there must have been a little bit of sentimentality. It was rarely noticeable, but when it showed it was always in this way.

Now, more than thirty years later, when I think about that little village, I regret that we did not understand how interesting it was. Linguists as well as archaeologists would have found much of interest. It was quite natural that it had not been discovered earlier. Tafonatu, so far as we could ascertain, is the only place from which it could be seen, and it had been ascended only twice before we got there. And besides, the valley was practically always filled with fog.[6]

---

6 In the autumn of 1937, I flew from Marseille to Ajaccio and passed over exactly those areas on the east side of Tafonatu, strangely enough in clear weather. Where in my opinion Valle Nebbio ought to have been, there was only a lake, from which a little river ran in torrents toward the coast. It is possible that in my haste I mistook the terrain, but it is also possible that a rockfall had blocked the narrow runoff from the meadow where the village was and that it now is under water, like so many such places.

Cinque Frati and Paglia Orba

We found our little campsite in perfect order. We lit a huge fire, bathed in the creek, ate, sunbathed, and made plans that day and the next. George thought we had to stick to being an alpine expedition – not an archaeological one – and as an alpine expedition it was our task to make ascents, preferably new ones, which were as difficult as possible. George was undeniably right.

Right above our campsite we had, as mentioned, Paglia Orba, an impressive-looking mountain from the position we were viewing it from, but one that is easy and simple to climb from the other side. A mountaineer does not get discouraged because the peak he wants to climb is easy to ascend from one side. Right away he finds another side, and it turns out that on almost any peak a mountaineer can bring himself into considerable difficulty and danger. We knew this would be so in the case of Paglia Orba when we attacked it from the south, the side facing our tent. The upper 1,500–1,800 feet looked to be practically vertical. From down below it is often difficult to judge where to take the path up a mountainside, and we therefore decided to prepare the ascent of Paglia Orba by first climbing the peaks of Cinque Frati on this side of the valley. From there we could study the south wall of Paglia Orba through binoculars and then make our plan for the trip.

We decided to start with the southernmost peak and then follow the ridge as far as possible until we came to the northernmost and highest one. To humour Max, our youngest member, George and I arranged that he should assume leadership of this expedition in return for carrying our entire luggage. That's how Max ended up with such a heavy backpack. George and I figured that with such good weather and Max carrying everything, we should bring ample provisions along to the top. From this we gleaned few pleasures.

It is common practice in mountain climbing to divide the dangers you encounter into subjective and objective categories: subjective dangers are those dangers you can think upon, and objective ones are those that nature and other people may expose you to, and about which there is nothing you can do one way or another.

Max went first during our climb up through a fairly steep fissure toward the top of the southernmost Frati, according to plan; George and I just let him go the whole length of the rope, partly because we had found a clever place to stand and smoke cigarettes. Once in a while we glanced up at a sixty- or seventy-degree angle and saw Max's backside, boot soles and part of his bird bag. Standing on a little shelf in a mountain wall, tied by rope to a man you can only see by his boot soles and the seat of his pants, can be quite nerve-racking. It is best not to have a lively imagination; if you spend your time painting pictures of how things would go if he lost his grip, you don't get anything near the 100 per cent benefit of the cigarette. Our imaginations meant that neither George nor I did.

We didn't exactly imagine we would get Max down on our heads, but little rocks now and then made our stay at the bottom of the fissure less peaceful than we would have wished. Our eyes followed Max with considerable self-interest. And then things began to unravel – literally. Somehow the string that closed his bird bag must have become caught in a crack. In any case, when Max was about 120–150 feet above us, the bag opened and started to pour our precious provisions all over us. We managed to catch the half-loaf of bread that came first, but after it a big jar of orange marmalade came sailing down. It is quite unpleasant to be standing at the bottom of a fissure while a jar of marmalade comes whistling down towards you. Even though you have filled your hat with crumpled-up paper – something you ought always to do if you have a novice climber above you on a mountain – this helps very little against a one-quart ceramic jar full of Crosse & Blackwell marmalade. Against such things you ought to be equipped with the now-popular steel helmet, but these were not on the market back then, and anyway you cannot walk around in a steel helmet for weeks just because of such a remote possibility.

About five feet above the little shelf where George and I were standing, the marmalade jar splashed against a protruding rock, where it lost a major part of its force and distributed its contents almost evenly over George and me.

After a while Max also became aware that all was not as it should be and tried, in spite of being somewhat constrained, to get hold of the opening in his bird bag. But he was also burdened by an ice axe that in some unfathomable manner was fastened to the back of his pack, and his effort to get hold of the bird bag string immediately resulted in the ice axe following the marmalade jar.

All this was very stressful for George and me as we could not get away from the fissure we were in without jerking the rope – which was now stretched almost all the way out – and getting all of Max and the rest of the equipment all over us.

We undeservedly escaped the attack of the ice axe when it somehow got caught just below Max. Considering the situation, we found it politically unwise to enter into a discussion with Max about what had happened, and we calmly continued after him up to the top, decorated in orange marmalade.

Once in the safety of the top of the southernmost of Cinque Frati, we explained to him in a straightforward manner that could not be misunderstood what we thought about his undoubtedly deliberate, cowardly attacks on his elders.

The rest of the trip across Cinque Frati passed without any particular event but gave us ample opportunity to use the rope, as all the peaks turned outwards to lean out and be perfectly smooth on the north side. The technique we used in descending from each peak across the passage between them was therefore always the same. Firstly, we sought out a suitable rock to put the rope around and lowered ourselves in a double rope. Then we pulled the rope down after us. In this way we finally reached the northernmost and highest of the five peaks and there we settled down with the remains of the provisions.

The weather was nice and clear and we had a great view toward the side of Paglia Orba we had thought to attack. We knew with approximate certainty that in order not to risk avalanches we could get as far up as the snow line, so long as we started early enough in the morning. But the last part of the mountain, some 900–1,200 feet or so, looked to be completely vertical. The possibility, if indeed there was one, had to be a kind of shelf in the shape of a big 'C' that reached in a curve from the top toward the left and down to a place where there was the highest patch of snow. We agreed to try that route.[1]

We took it easy again the next day, but the morning after that we were on our feet before sunup and soon were kicking our way up the steep snowbanks that stretched up the east face of Paglia Orba.

After a while we also had a closer impression of the topography and saw that we could get up to a sharp snow ridge between a protrusion in the mountainside and the vertical face of the mountain itself. We settled down where we were, ate, drank, smoked cigarettes and discussed the future. It looked dark and steep. It turned out that the whole face of the mountain now before us, and which covered the shelf we had planned to get to, hung out so that bits of ice, small rocks and other loose elements that slithered out from the top ridge fell freely, without touching the mountainside until reaching the approximate level of where we found ourselves. For the remaining part of the climb this was a great advantage: there is nothing more nerve-racking than being involved in difficult climbing with gravel and bits of ice constantly whistling around your ears.

From where we were standing up to the lowest part of the shelf there was clearly a steep rock face, but never steeper than vertical. There was also some ice in the runnels and cracks. That caused us quite a bit of bother but also provided quite a bit of help.

---

1   It was later revealed to us that the Austrian mountain climber Albert Gerngross along with a Swiss guide had made an unsuccessful attempt at climbing Paglia Orba up that same route in 1907.

On the last stretch of rock up to the lowest part of the shelf we were headed for, we had to go up through a deep, slippery and completely vertical fissure, the lower part of which was filled with ice. Had this not been the case, it would probably have been exceptionally difficult to ascend. As things stood, we could chop steps into the ice and then get up by one man standing at the top of the ice stairs and pressing against the fissure, while the next man climbed on him and stood on his shoulders until he reached a serviceable hold.

Once we had done this, we were finally up on the shelf we had seen from Cinque Frati two days earlier. It slanted out over the precipice to the left of where we were standing and was, as I mentioned, completely sheltered by the overhanging precipice some several hundred feet above it. In some places the shelf was interrupted by deep fissures, several of which we had to climb fairly far down into in order to get over to the other side and up to the continuation of the shelf.

After a few hours we finally reached the point where the 'C' turned and went on up to the right. The impression we had of this place from seeing it from Cinque Frati was that there we would come over to a snow or ice fissure which we fairly easily could chop our way up. It turned out to be completely different – the shelf we were walking on became narrower and narrower and was finally no more than about a foot wide between two vertical walls. This edge also stopped abruptly right where we thought the worst would be over. We then saw that what we had thought was a snow fissure in reality was a kind of frozen waterfall, clearly formed in the course of winter by water trickling down from the passage above, and which now reached down a bit below the shelf where we were standing. It ended in a row of icicles that hung down into empty space. I think the width of this icefall was 120–150 feet and it was very steep, maybe sixty degrees, to the part of it we could reach.

The situation was such that we thought we should give it serious consideration. We knew that with enough patience and endurance we should be able to chop steps diagonally up the icefall and get to a rock outcropping on the other side. It looked as if we ought to be able to continue from there. The question that concerned us most, however, was whether the icefall would hold. It was not, as mentioned, like ordinary ice fissures that usually have some sort of support from below – it simply hung freely out over the rock wall. It was not possible for us to determine if the whole thing would crack and fall down with all of us when we had chopped a suitable number of steps in it.

I think it was almost laziness that made us decide to continue. We knew it was a heavy, long and trying trip back if we turned around. If we got across the icefall, it looked as if we would quite quickly get all the way to the top and have an easy way back down to the tent.

It was slow and heavy work chopping steps across this ice. Luckily the ice was completely hard and firm, but that did not make step-chopping any easier. Because of the steepness it was necessary to first chop very big steps for our boots and then a hold for our right hand. All this had to be done with only the left arm using the ice axe.

We went across from the end of that shelf diagonally up to the rock outcropping on the other side of the icefall at an average speed of thirty feet per hour. It took exactly three hours to go the ninety-foot length of rope it turned out to require.

I don't know for whom those three hours were the most exciting: for George and Max, who sat on the granite shelf with a quite precarious anchorage, or for me, who was doing the step-chopping work. I think that it really must have been most exciting for George and Max, but there is no doubt that it was most trying for me.

Once safely across to the rock outcropping, I straddled it, got hold of some chocolate and cigarettes I had in my pocket, and yelled, 'All clear!' to those who were waiting below. As I hauled in the rope, first one then the other head popped up over the edge of the ice. I cannot say we bid farewell to the icefall with any kind of regret. It would have been fun to see that whole mass of ice rush out over the 900–1,200-foot precipice below it and on down the rock wall, but annoying if we had been carried along.

As we had predicted, the difficult parts of the ascent were now over. After about an hour of easy climbing up the rock wall, we reached the peak just as the sun in the west sank into the Mediterranean.[2]

Paglia Orba is an ideal mountain to descend at that time of year because the entire west side is covered by nice snow mounds about as steep as a normal ski jump. You have only to sit down, put the ice axe under your arm for steering and thus you get down in incredibly short time, although not so fast as the well-known, dead mountain climber in the Dolomite Alps on whose headstone is written:

Den Aufstieg macht'er in 7 Stunden,
aber in 3 Secunden
war er unten.[3]

Laziness overcame us again the next morning. It was often that way for us when we had been energetic for a few days. There may have been an opportunity to make many more pleasant trips from that campsite in Valle Calasima but, as I said, we had become too idle. We spent the next day sunbathing and eating most of the remaining provisions, and then we broke camp the following morning and sauntered down to get back to Calacuccia. We had experienced a lot in the week since we walked up that same road, and still had a lot to talk about on the way down.

As we came around one of the mountain ridges that come down from the south of Cinque Frati, we were suddenly on the outskirts of the Calasima village.

'Dammit to hell,' said George. 'We were not supposed to come here. Our patient is probably dead by now and that could be a nuisance.'

---

2 The only later ascent of Paglia Orba from the same side that I've been able to discover was done in 1932 by Walter Amstutz with the well-known Swiss guide Risch. They did not follow our route, which can hardly be used except in quite exceptional snow and ice conditions. Amstutz and Risch went up a ridge south of the one we followed and at the top of it they came to the same spot that we had reached after having chopped our way across the icefall (*Alpine Journal,* May 1933).

3 'He made the ascent in seven hours, but came back down in three seconds.'

It was too late to change our minds. Some of the people on the outskirts of the village had already seen us and were announcing our arrival with loud cries. This did not give us an encouraging impression. 'I hope we won't be forced to take part in the funeral,' said George.

We took a good grip on the ice axes and trooped into the main street. However, our dire predictions about the results of our doctoring activities turned out to be quite superfluous. The priest met us outside his house along with the patient, who was in the peak of health. She looked decidedly better than last time, and the priest also said the cure had been almost instantaneous. Improvement had been detected from the very first day, and the priest then had thought it reasonable to increase the dosage somewhat, he said. After three days the patient had declared herself cured and refused any more medicine. How this could be I've never been able to see, but I find it less than believable that by our experiment we should have discovered a quick and effective cure for tuberculosis. It is more probable that the woman was not sick at all but had seen an advantage in playing the patient. Healthy women in Corsica are exploited in heavy labour to an extensive degree. With that in mind, the cure may be explained by the fact that faced with two ills the sufferer will choose the lesser of the two.

We still had a considerable stock of Sagrada laxative pills. As I already mentioned, it was for some inexplicable reason the only medicine for internal use we had brought along from Switzerland. As our experience until now had convinced us we did not need them, we left the rest of our stock with the priest and asked him to use them to the best of his ability should there be more cases of illness in his village.

The priest had probably been aware of how things stood the whole time. He smiled conspiratorially and said that the mere knowledge of his possession of large amounts of medication would probably keep the village population healthy for a long time to come. As a thank you for our medical assistance he gave us a large brown and green glazed ceramic jar from the district's own production, a present we were only modestly pleased with

– especially Max, who, of course, had the honour of carrying it. We told the priest a little about the village on the other side of Tafonatu and had hoped to learn a bit more about it, but that was useless. What we told him – which really wasn't very much – did not seem to interest him in the least. 'So many people live in the mountains,' he said. 'We cannot know them all.'

We ate goat at the priest's and continued down to Hotel de France in Calacuccia in the afternoon.

Bandits

In the middle of the night three days later, we walked in the pitch dark on an almost invisible path up through the *macchia* on the south side of the Calacuccia valley in the direction of Monte Rotondo. It was overcast and visibility did not extend farther than the small amount of terrain that was illuminated by two small, bad lanterns. Ahead of us was Carlo Bonelli, a valued member of one of Corsica's best-known bandit organisations at that time.

Our plan had really been to walk from Calacuccia across the mountains to the town of Corte, make a few excursions in those areas, and then take the train to Ajaccio and back to France by boat. But things don't always go according to plan – on the contrary, things usually go quite differently and this is really a great blessing. If everything went according to plan, you would first experience a series of things of the utmost discomfort, for example those times when others make nasty plans against you. Besides, you would miss almost all experiences of any value – first of all because you rarely have enough imagination to plan anything really fun, and secondly because a whole lot of the amusing things you experience by coincidence become more fun and more welcome precisely because they were not planned. This does not mean that you should not make plans and work to realise them – on the contrary, the work of making a plan and realising it is always fun, even if the result is of no great value. Besides, haphazard events seem both more humorous and more haphazard when they occur as a break in a carefully made and practically executed plan. Our entire expedition to Corsica stemmed from the coincidence of my being present at the little variety show in Zurich just that evening when George gave his boxing performance there, and most of what we experienced during the expedition was also related to coincidence rather than keeping to the plans we had made.

The fact that we were now wandering in the pitch dark up toward Monte Rotondo with a Corsican bandit was an indirect result of the coincidence of George and me finding James the snake a few weeks earlier on our way home to Hotel de France in Calacuccia. That story had strangely enough made us extraordinarily popular in what you may call wide circles, meaning first of all with the host at the hotel and then with a large part of his family and friends. All of these people cooperated with those groups of bandits that lived in the districts south and west of Monte Rotondo and Monte d'Oro.

At this point it is natural to give a brief introduction to Corsican bandits. The first thing to note is that the designation *bandito*, as it is used in Corsica, does not have the same meaning as the word 'bandit' has come to have in Italian and many other languages. The designation *bandito* is used in Corsica in the original sense of the word: someone who has been banned or excommunicated. There is a sharp distinction between *bandito* and *brigante*, which means robber.

Approximate parallels to Corsican bandits would be figures like Robin Hood, Gunnar of Lidarende and the Chieftain of Gønge. All of these were bandits in the same vein as the Corsican ones – they had come afoul of the powers that be for one reason or another and lived as someone who has been excommunicated. This kind of bandit will always exist when a country's legal system does not provide sufficient assurance that a crime will be punished, or if the powers that be proclaim laws that run counter to the common perception of the law. We have excellent examples of the latter in the laws about prohibition, which at the time of their attempted implementation met with little success in Norway and America, among others. As we know, they led directly and indirectly to the development of a true class of organised *banditos*, which stood outside the law but which were more or less clearly supported by the major part of the population.

The *banditos*, as we know from Norway and Iceland's old history, developed primarily as a result of an inadequate legal system. Their basic perception of the law gave them the right to take the law into their own hands when there was no officialdom to do so. The bandit life in Corsica developed along approximately the same lines. Most of those who became bandits in the last 100 years did so because of vendettas.

I have earlier specifically touched on the Corsican vendetta at the end of the chapter on Corsican history, but it deserves a more thorough discussion in the context of the nature of the Corsican banditry to which the vendetta[1] has been the most important contributor. The 'vendetta' is often translated in Norwegian as 'blood vengeance', but this translation is not quite correct. A vendetta does not necessarily result in murder, it is simply a designation for taking the law into one's own hands. It becomes rather obvious that for the one who is to exercise justice and act as prosecutor, judge and upholder of the law in his own case, it becomes natural to take simple and effective measures when faced with real or claimed insult. Under such circumstances the case is usually such that the injured party, just to make sure, provides quite an ample portion of revenge. Even if he does not necessarily in the first instance resort to murder, it does not take long for that stage to be reached.

The history of Norway also provides abundant examples of rapidly mounting degrees of provocation and retaliation. A case might have developed in which a female member of a family insulted a female member of another family, whereupon the husband of the latter beat to death the servant of the former. This was then vindicated by the first one setting fire to the other's house

---

1 When ordinary dictionaries say that the word vendetta is derived from the Latin word *vindicare*, that is a simple but certainly incorrect explanation – something that comparative linguistics has long since established. Gregorovius' hypothesis about the word being of Germanic origin and the same root as the German word *fehme* does not seem to be valid. Far more reasonable is the Icelandic researcher Vilhjalmur Jonson's theory that the word came from the Old Norse *hefnidetr*. This theory has been further strengthened by the discovery of a grave from around 1100, which was made at the end of the 1920s. Among the remains from Sigurd Jorsalsfar's stay in Corsica, several inscriptions were found containing the word in runic characters.

and the next step was then a regular life-and-death feud between two families or two groups of families. A regulated legal system may sometimes also have its disadvantages, at least for some, but it does have the aspect of deterring such a rapid progression, and in some instances the punishment suits the crime.

The Corsicans must generally have been very sensitive. Not much was needed before a vendetta was started.[2] This may also be related to the fear of being regarded as cowardly if you didn't immediately and thoroughly avenge whatever might be seen as an insult.

One incident that is typical of the development of the Corsican vendetta took place in 1822. The inhabitants of two neighbouring villages were gathered on the evening before Easter in a common religious procession. They walked to a nearby chapel with the bell-ringer at the head, followed by the priests with holy images. In the middle of the road the procession came upon a cadaver of a mule and the bell-ringer accused the inhabitants of one of the villages, Borgo, of having placed the cadaver there. Borgo's inhabitants were extremely insulted by this accusation and claimed that it was the inhabitants of the other village, Lucciana, who were responsible for the mule cadaver. The religious procession was immediately abandoned. The priests stopped singing *Ave Maria* and the people started shooting and fighting. The inhabitants of Borgo pushed back the people of Lucciana, took the mule cadaver along and placed it in front of the church door in Lucciana. But then the happy war changed – the inhabitants of Lucciana forced their way into Borgo and pulled the mule cadaver up on to Borgo's church spire. This event provided the opportunity for a vendetta feud that led to a series of murders.

In the course of about a year both villages had been levelled and the few survivors continued their lives as bandits. When the vendetta had developed as far as the first murder, the transition to

---

2 You get an impression of the extent of the Corsican vendetta when you hear that a Corsican historian estimates the number of victims of vendetta killings in the period from 1359 to 1729 to have been 330,000. After 1729 the numbers decreased and were calculated to be approximately 70,000. The yearly average over the past 600 years has been approximately 700. The population of Corsica in 1750 was 120,000, and in 1850 it was 250,000.

the bandit life has started inasmuch as the murderer not only has the murder victim's family after him but also the powers that be. He then finds his way up into the *macchia* in the uninhabited and inaccessible mountain areas, where the bandit groups have been staying since Sampiero's and Paoli's days, when they made up the core of the national troops who fought against the island's various foreign masters.

As the vendetta automatically led to a continuous renewal of these elements of obstruction, various governments on their part attempted over time to stop or limit it. Stiff punishment was administered, not just for the one who committed the vendetta murder but also for those who encouraged it or chastised others because they did not sufficiently avenge an injustice that concerned someone in the family. In Corsica there is a word for accusing another person of not executing revenge severely enough. It is called *rimbeccare*.

Under Genoese rule of Corsica it was first decided that, by law, anyone guilty of *rimbecco* must be imprisoned for an undetermined length of time. When even this did not work, it was decided that as extra punishment the guilty party should have his tongue pierced in a public place of execution. It does not seem that these decisions about punishment measures worked – even stronger measures were instituted against bandits who had retreated after the murder of one or more private or public persons. Not only were they the bandits hunted relentlessly, but also family members and friends of the bandits in question were allegedly placed in prison, where they would then stay until the bandits turned themselves over to the authorities of their own free will. Yet even these measures, which one would think were sufficiently severe, could not bring the bandits to heel.

In this connection it is interesting to point out that as late as 1931, the French police conducted a regular war against the bandits in the mountain areas around Monte Rotondo.

That the bandits could keep going for as long as they did, in spite of the continuing struggle against their enemies among the population as well as the military and the police, is of course related to the fact that they were supported by large parts of the population. In the course of the nineteenth century the big bandit families, such as Spada, Bonelli and Romanetti, also gained political influence by their connections within the population and probably also by a certain amount of terror that they wielded, which would produce votes, decisive for one candidate or another in local elections or for the Chamber of Deputies.[3] The bandit families also always had relatives or friends brought into trusted positions in the police and customs services, so that they were always well informed about what was about to happen.

After Corsica came under French rule, the bandits were rarely subjected to any energetic pursuit, except for a few incidents when one of their political candidates was beaten by his opponent.

Our leader on the night expedition south from Calacuccia belonged, as already mentioned, to the Bonelli family, one of the most influential of the bandit families at the time, although not the oldest.

The first Bonelli to become a *bandito* lived at the beginning of the nineteenth century and was a well-off farmer in the area north of Ajaccio. In his youth this Bonelli, whose name was Torres, was a Don Juan of considerable dimensions. Because of his well-shaped legs, he was given the name Bellacoccia.

In the village of Vizzavona, where the Bonelli family lived, there was also another family, Simonetti, with three daughters: Josephine, Désirée and Letitia. (The family was clearly inspired by Bonaparte.) Torres began a relationship with the oldest Simonetti girl, Josephine, not because he liked her any better than the others but because according to the custom of the place you should always start with the oldest of a family's unmarried daughters. It is said of the sisters Josephine, Désirée and Letitia that they were always particularly good friends. The further developments of this story would show that this was truly the case.

---

3   Prince Jerome Napoleon was elected to the Chamber of Deputies as the representative for the district of Ajaccio in May of 1876, allegedly because of the influence of the Bonelli family.

Torres Bonelli was not in possession of the same patient nature as Jacob, who toiled for seven years for his Rachel. On the contrary, Torres waited only a few months before he arranged things with Désirée, and in less than six months he was, to put it mildly, courting all three.

Aside from his advantageous physical attributes he must also have possessed considerable diplomatic tact, because it is said that for a long time each of the sisters thought she was the only one to be going steady with Torres. Needless to say, this could not work in the long run. Because of one unexpected accident or another, the three sisters were suddenly made aware of the whole picture. To give Torres a fitting surprise, all three of them showed up for a tryst he had arranged with just one of them. It seems to me that this must have been a fairly embarrassing situation. Not one you would want to be in.

Torres, as we know, had considerable diplomatic abilities, and in spite of everything he managed to bring harmony into this strange foursome. The three Simonetti sisters, who must have been lovely people, continued to be the good friends they had always been and agreed that thirty-three per cent of Torres, when all was said and done, was preferable to a hundred per cent of any other available bachelor in the village.

All would have been well if the sisters had not also had a brother. He was informed of the triple alliance through rumour, which will always sooner or later appear in such cases. He thought the case blighted the Simonetti family honour. The brother sought out Torres, and it is said that on this occasion comments of an injurious nature were exchanged, so injurious even that Torres a short time later found it necessary to shoot the young Simonetti.

Thereby his fate was sealed. Torres had to get away from the village and into the *macchia*. With the three sisters he went up into one of the mountain valleys on the south side of Monte Rotondo and there established himself among the bandits of the Spada and Romanetti families, who already had their place in these areas. He lived a happy family life with Josephine, Désirée and Letitia and with them had forty children, of which twenty-four were sons.

As is customary, a few of these sons were sent to school in Ajaccio and after a while entered police and customs services.

It is said that Torres married all three of the sisters, but this can hardly be true as both the Bonelli and Simonetti families were Orthodox Catholics. As we know, in the Catholic faith polygamy is not permitted.[4] It is more reasonable to think that Torres let the two younger Simonetti sisters be formally married to two of his younger brothers, a method widely used by Corsican bandits to make sure their children would have a bourgeois education and not be subjected to any hardship because of their fathers' misdeeds.

The sons who stayed with him up in the mountains were busy defending and attacking and committing a series of vendetta murders. By their twenties, several of the sons had been sentenced to death, some as many as four times.

The Bonellis who lived in the mountains and narrow valleys on the west side of Monte Rotondo were in close contact with the other bandit families, Spada and Romanetti, and exercised strong and wide influence.

As I mentioned earlier, it was James the snake that had put us in touch with Carlo Bonelli. It was during these days of the Easter break that the preparations for a very exciting election campaign were taking place, and it was the municipal elections in the arrondissement of Ajaccio, Bocognano and Corte that were of interest to the bandit colonies. These municipalities border the mountain areas where the biggest groups of bandits live. For the candidates not supported by the bandits, it was important to discredit or neutralise them before the elections. To that end they had allied themselves with the police authorities in Bastia (the police in Ajaccio and Corte belonged to the other party).

The two police agents with whom we had kept such good company at Hotel de France a few weeks earlier were out to secure the help of informants in various villages around the bandit areas,

---

4 See Martin Luther and Philip Melanchthon's dogmatic exposé in connection with Count Philip of Hesse's double marriage.

in the hope that there would be raids with the help of police troops not connected to the bandits.

In the meantime, the story involving James had been brilliantly exploited for political agitation with the help of the hotel host's extensive circle of acquaintances, and had provided the bandits and their candidates with that most powerful and dangerous ally in political conflicts: laughter. Faced with that kind of opponent, the police agents who were bandit enemies could accomplish nothing. All in all there was, according to what the hotel host told us, much to indicate that James, in this case, had represented the balance on the scale.

We had spent the evening of our return to Calacuccia with our host and Bonelli. In the course of the evening we had heard the description by Carlo Bonelli of his family and family life as bandits, all the way from his great-grandfather – the original Bonelli bandit of the three wives – going up into the mountains. Carlo himself was not a bandit, but he held a position of confidence in bandit circles and seemed obviously to be a kind of ambassador or go-between vis-à-vis the authorities. At that time he was in his thirties and had received an excellent education, partly in Ajaccio and partly in France, and seemed like a cultivated man of the world.

Carlo was the only one of the Corsicans we met who immediately understood us when we told of our interest in mountain climbing. He asked with interest about the situation in Norway and Australia and was especially interested to know if we also had *banditos* as in Corsica. It was quite embarrassing to have to admit that there was not a great deal of that. The only thing I could serve up were the now somewhat old-fashioned stories of farm weddings in Hemsedal with stabbings and duels and such, but as expected this did not impress him very much. George and Max were more favourably placed, with their big, unexplored areas within their country's borders. But Bonelli knew at least as much about these things as George and Max, so there could be no doubt who the winner was in this competition between nations.

Before parting for the evening, we were invited to accompany Bonelli across the mountains and down to the family enclave in one of the valleys on the south-west side of Monte Rotondo. That is the way the plans for the last part of our Corsica expedition were changed.

We spent the next day packing and sending back to Switzerland all the things we no longer needed, and far into the night we set out in the pitch dark. Our friend Carlo insisted on that. He was a kind and trustworthy type, but he really wanted no one to have any knowledge of the route into the mountains.

At daybreak we were already on our way down the south slope of the first mountain chain we had to traverse. We came to the un-inhabited part of Valle Tavignano, and in its upper reaches we made camp at around lunch time.

Our friend Carlo was a careful general; he could find his way in the dark, making it unnecessary to walk in the daytime. It was a somewhat unusual way to hike, but not without its charms. Among other things you sleep more comfortably and better in the grass in the warm sun than at night in a few degrees of frost.

Around two o'clock in the morning we got up and made coffee. Carlo made the fire in a narrow cleft between two stone cliffs, and every once in a while he glanced up toward one of the rifts in the rock wall on the south side of the valley. After a while we saw a faint light there. Carlo walked back and forth in front of the cleft, stopping from time to time, sometimes directly between the fire and the other light, sometimes to the side. The other light answered these signals in the same way.

'Everything in order,' said Carlo. 'I have warned them ahead of time that I expected to arrive with guests, but there is always some kind of control, particularly in the times just before election days. This trail, however, is almost never used. It is difficult to find.'

In the course of the night we must have crossed the ridge between Monte Rotondo and Artica at an altitude of about 6,000 feet. The terrain was steep on the south side but not so steep that we had to make any real effort climbing, which was just as well as we only had the faint light from two bad lanterns and carried considerable baggage.

As day began to dawn, we were down in the upper reaches of

forest, some 3,800–3,900 feet above sea level. To our left were a series of mountain ridges that ran west from the Rotondo massif, and now we could see how the fog was formed in these western valley areas. It came seeping in with the east wind down from all the rifts and depressions in the highest ridge that separated the east and west land masses, filled the valleys like some kind of avalanche and then evaporated as it came down toward warmer layers of air. That must have been the way Valle Nebbio was filled, but there the fog stayed because the valley had practically no outlet.

The Bonelli headquarters were located on a shelf in one of the many narrow valleys. For the most part these valleys are narrow canyons between almost vertical mountains many hundreds of feet high, but in some places there are open fields where the river or stream runs fairly peacefully through the terrain before cutting into the cliffs again.

It was not a village but a series of clusters of stone houses spread out among chestnut and fir trees. The place was particularly full of chestnut trees. The old Bellacoccia, Torres, had planted the first trees, and after about a hundred years of complete lack of care or treatment these eager trees had developed into an entire forest that nourished the whole colony – and its pigs. These animals, along with chestnuts and goats, were the main resources in these areas, probably because they manage on their own and do not give people unnecessary bother. The Bonelli colony was therefore, like the Nebbio village, autonomous as far as food provision was concerned, and this must have been of a certain importance at times.

The tribal chief – Torres Bonelli, the original Torres grandson – lived in the biggest stone house. It was a large, solid house, obviously placed and built with an eye toward defence. That was also how it had been used on many occasions for generations. From a small porch we entered a spacious, nicely furnished living room – whitewashed walls, the floor made of wide fir boards, dark beams in the ceiling, a big fireplace in one of the long walls and big, heavy furniture made of chestnut wood stained a dark colour. The room was a little dark for us until we became used to the change of light, but that ended quickly.

At the end of the long table sat the head of the family – Torres Bonelli. I had been very excited about this meeting, not only because of his reputation as a bandit, but also because I, during the hike across the mountains in the dark, had had the idea that I was certainly related to him. It was the similarity between the names Torres Bonelli and Tørris Bonnevie (my great-great-grandfather's half-brother on the mother's side), in connection with my awareness that the Bonnevie family originally came from these Mediterranean areas, that gave me the idea. It was also known that Tørris Bonnevie had returned to Norway at the end of the eighteenth century after having made a considerable fortune elsewhere.

As a result of the youthful urge to hero worship, he was seen by the younger members of the family to have been a pirate; and what could have been more natural than conducting this activity from a base in Corsica, and being connected to that branch of his family that he had met there? Besides, how could the name Torres otherwise have come to Corsica? It is certainly not an Italian first name. As we know, the name Tørris comes from the Nedenes family, who had it from Jutland in Denmark.

Later studies have reinforced my belief in the idea I had back then based on intuition about the connection between Tørris Bonnevie and the Corsican Bonelli family. From my family's chronicles (*The Bonnevie Family in Norway and Denmark*, Johan Grundt Tanum Publishers, Oslo) it appears that Tørris Bonnevie was captured by a pirate ship in 1793. Because this probably happened in the Mediterranean while Tørris was on his way to the south of France, it seems evident that he at this time ended up with his Corsican relatives. When the family chronicles say that he then in the course of a few years amassed a considerable fortune in 'commerce and shipping', one might safely assume that these words say it in a nice way. I do not belong among those who object to the possibility of being able, by legal means, to amass a fortune in commerce and shipping, but I think that all those who have tried it will admit that it is more quickly accomplished through smuggling and piracy.

Be all that as it may, I had decided to take a firm stand on the question of the family, largely to get the better of George and Max, who were particularly well situated because of their snake-charming abilities.

As I now had the opportunity to look more closely at our host, it seemed to me that he had a considerable likeness to many of our family portraits, but this may also have been based on imagination or faulty memory. Family or no family, we were in any case extra-ordinarily well received by Uncle Torres. After the story of James the snake, we belonged under all circumstances to the party members.

Torres Bonelli was proud of his house, and not without reason. It was, as I mentioned, an old, solid house originally built as a fort. From the cellar there was an underground passage leading to a rift in the mountain several hundred feet away. It must have taken many years of energetic labour to make it, and on two separate occasions it had saved the Bonellis from the clutches of their attackers, who had managed to surround their place of residence. You could therefore say that the work invested in this passage had paid off.

For George, Max and me it was the first time we had met real bandits on their private turf, and it cannot be denied that it seemed to us a very curious experience. The experience was not so un-conventional as we had thought, something a better knowledge of the history of Corsican banditry would have shown us. However, we lacked this knowledge then, just as we were ignorant of just about everything to do with Corsica. In fact, at the time we were there and for a long time before that, it was not at all an unusual thing for bandits to receive visits by tourists.

In the book *Korsika och Tunis* by Otto Hjelt, published in 1882, Hjelt describes in detail a visit to two Bonelli family brothers who lived on the Pentico mountain on the south-west side of Monte Rotondo, not far from the colony where we were staying. During the flowering of tourism as a source of income in the 1920s, these visits to the various bandit families were organised on an almost commercial basis. For a period of time, and for an additional fee, it was not unheard of to include a visit to the bandits in the excursions arranged by travel agencies.

That is the way it had been during those periods when the bandits were not subject to any urgent pursuit by the authorities – meaning during those periods when their own political parties were in power. The strife that existed during such periods was reduced to internal, private feuds between bandit families and between the bandits and particular enemies in various villages.

A considerable part of the shooting that took place was certainly also arranged to please the visiting tourists – along the same principles as the famous 'apache' dancers in the seedy parts of Paris, where in the old days tourists had the opportunity to witness the most upsetting jealousy-and-revenge dramas between the 'apaches'.

Our visit to the Bonellis took place during a peaceful period. The authorities in practically all the surrounding municipalities had been elected many years before, with the help of bandit votes and influence. It was, in fact, only the circumstances of the up-coming elections that caused guard posts and other security measures to be installed.

Although the Bonelli colony was located in an inaccessible mountain area and cut off from any connection to the outside world, it was in possession of a first-class information system. This had existed for a long time and had been developed on the basis of the optical telegraph (heliograph), which Napoleon I used between the Spanish border and Paris, among other things. The Bonelli colony had a very simple and effective signal connection with a trusted man in the Gravone valley near Bocagnano. From one of the mountains about halfway to the Gravone valley you had an unobstructed view of the Bonelli colony toward the north and the Bocagnano district toward the south.

Some of the younger members of the family always stayed in a little cabin on this mountainside. At certain times, usually just before sunrise and right after sunset, the day's news arrived by Morse code from Bocagnano via this mountain cabin down to the Bonelli headquarters.

Uncle Torres was obviously a man with an interest in technical improvements and was very proud of a signal receptor of his own invention. This consisted of long maritime binoculars, permanently directed toward the window opening in the mountain cabin some fifteen miles away. At signal time you had only to sit by the binoculars and pay attention. If conditions for reception were good, you did not even look through the binoculars. A little piece of thin paper in front of the lens was enough to show the flashes of light.

During the evening we spent at Bonelli's, the message arrived about the election results, which had gone in Bonelli's favour, and this created a great atmosphere. For George, Max and me this was really a much stranger experience than we were anticipating. It was our first encounter with the wireless telegraph (even ultra shortwave).

Time passed quickly that evening with stories of the bandits' lives and with our own stories, particularly those about our different experiences in Corsica. The story about James the snake had to be told many times, and I think it got better with each telling.

Late in the evening I took up the question of family relations. I told Torres the story of Tørris and his stay in Corsica at the end of the eighteenth century. It fell on receptive, some might even say excellent, ears. In the Bonelli family the name Torres had been unknown before 1800. This was decidedly the atmosphere in which to ascertain that it had been started by Tørris exactly in those years when he had lived here. It might even be that he was godfather to the already mentioned Bellacoccia.

George and Max were sceptical for a moment toward this family relationship, which, as I had calculated, put me in a privileged position. But they were soon aware that this was an effort at general happiness and usefulness, and that they themselves would also benefit. After a while we felt as if we were members of an extended family and became disposed to further divulge our activities.

As far as our visit to Valle Nebbio was concerned, we had agreed to stay quite reticent. At first we had the impression that the story for some reason was not popular, nor did it illicit much interest. But as the evening progressed, we came around to it, and here we were not met with any kind of disbelief. On the contrary, the description brought immediate interest and brought about an exchange of comments among the Bonellis that was completely unintelligible to us. At first we were not quite sure what kind of impression the story had made, but it was not long before we realised that it first and foremost created humour.

'Oh really,' said the chief. 'You have visited Nini. It has been a long time since I saw her. Tell me how that old crackpot is doing.'

It cannot be denied that this at first had the effect of a cold shower, but then we remembered that the old mayoress, as we had called her, in reality belonged to the Bonelli family – perhaps she was our present host's aunt. (Later it turned out that the family relationship was not that close. The mayoress' father had been married to a cousin of our host's grandfather.)[5] We told him that Nini seemed to be doing well and that we had had an excellent time there for a few days.

'Nice girls at Nini's,' said one of the younger boys. We agreed with him in a polite way.

'Oh, that Nini,' said our host. 'She is true to herself. A terrible braggart, but a great person. And she lives in a good location. We and a few of our closest friends are practically the only people who can find our way there.

'We usually retreat to Nini's if there is something really wrong going on. Once you've arrived at Nini's you disappear from the world, so to speak, and can be in hiding there for months and have a great time.'

'And there's so much good food,' said one of the boys.

'And so many nice girls,' said the one who had said it once before. He obviously belonged to the type whose taste is more aesthetic than culinary.

'Well,' said our host, 'not everything Nini said was bragging. It was quite true that her father was the first to discover that village, and she did grow up there. But later she went out into the world, performed in a series of variety shows in France and was finally

---

5   In other words, it is not unthinkable that Nini really was my great aunt.

married to a hotelier in Marseille. When her husband died, she ran the hotel for a few years and also had a night cafe. Then she got tired of it and decided to return to Nebbio.

'To make a really good impression on the inhabitants there she brought the stone head of a ram she had bought and which we had a really hard time transporting there. Your certainly saw it down there.'

Oh, yes, we had seen it, but had thought it was an old Phoenician sculpture.

'Yes, that may well be,' said Bonelli, 'but she did buy it in Marseille. After she came back, some of us lived at her place for a while until she got everything organised and since then everything has been fine. But we never talk about Nebbio here because it is not good to have the place be too well known. We usually call it "chez Nini". That was the name she gave the little night cafe she had in Marseille.'

I have since pondered quite a lot about how my supposed relatives in Corsica managed to acquire sufficient income to maintain as high a standard of living as they had. As far as food and drink were concerned, we couldn't have had better on our visit, even though the diet would have become monotonous in the long run. The guest rooms we were offered were in every respect preferable to any we had experienced in hotels.

It was obvious that the colony at that time received considerable cash income in the form of political subsidies, but as we later were able to ascertain they also had considerable income from smuggling merchandise such as tobacco, saccharin and heroin into France.[6] It has in the past been easy to organise that kind of activity via Corsica.

---

6   It is interesting to note that heroin at that time was already regarded as an attractive narcotic, although Professor Willstätter around the turn of the century had proved that it was a completely harmless drug and had introduced it as preventive medicine against whooping cough. I personally knew about this because in Zurich I lived in the same boarding house as Willstätter's assistant, Dr Freudenreich. It was on the latter's initiative that during the whooping cough epidemic in 1908 we had heroin mixed with sugar on our morning porridge and thereby every one of us came unscathed through that period of illness.

To someone who appreciates a nice stay with good food with lovely hosts in idyllic settings, the kind of visit we paid to the Bonelli colony is ideal. George, however, was of another opinion. First of all he had little or no interest in family gossip, and that was quite reasonable inasmuch as it was not his family it concerned. Secondly, both he and Max had imagined the whole thing differently. If you have been expecting a hectic get-together with robbers and murderers, it must be surprising, not to mention disappointing, when it turns out you've landed in something that brings to mind a missionary meeting with tea and crumpets.

It wasn't that George hadn't tried. While I was wasting time (according to George) with nice talk about possible mutual relatives and acquaintances, he had brought up the question of participation in one ongoing vendetta strife or another with the younger members of the colony, or possibly coming along to start another. But here he came up against polite but insurmountable resistance. Although it was true that there was still an excellent vendetta going on between the Bonellis and the Simonettis in Vizzavona, it was the Simonettis who had the right to take the initiative. The last murder had been committed by two of the Bonelli brothers more than a year ago, so from their side the account was fully settled.

It so happened that the Bonellis for the time being had a surplus in the vendetta. It would be completely contrary to good form to now hit the war path, nor could they count on any kind of attack, the way the elections had turned out. As well as all of this, it would to a high degree damage the family's prestige to include strangers in a vendetta. We had ended up in an exceedingly exclusive society and the new addition to the vendetta technique, which I was convinced that George would be able to launch, found no opportunity to make itself felt. I think the visit at the Bonellis' was the only really big disappointment that George experienced in Corsica.

The next day we travelled on. With our old friend Carlo as pathfinder we passed the nearest mountain ridges to the south, and through a fantastically narrow passage we eventually came down to one of the upper villages in the Liamone valley. This was one of the smallest villages we saw in Corsica. To make up for that, it was called Scanafaggiaccia. We spent the night at the priest's, who was a good friend of Carlo's.

A few days later we found ourselves on Promenade des Anglais in Nice. We had spent a day in Ajaccio[7] and had taken the boat in the evening. It cannot be denied that we were less presentable than we thought we looked. We caused considerable attention too, and had the impression it was not especially flattering. But that was not so strange.

When we started our trip two months earlier, our clothes had been worn and well used, but generally intact. Now we were dressed in shreds and rags that only with the help of strategically placed safety pins could be arranged to cover our most essential parts (whatever those may be).

For George the situation had its bright side. In his mind he already saw us in a fight with a selection of Nice's tourists and natives, whose comments about our outfits could very well be seen as insulting and thereby lead to complications. To mine and Max's great relief I succeeded this time in calming his contentiousness and got him to understand that the situation had to be taken into consideration.

The situation (and here I mean the financial one) was in no way bright. Altogether we had twenty-seven and a half francs – including three fake five-lire pieces – about 200 francs less than what we needed for the cheapest tickets back to Zurich. We had to get back as soon as possible because the school authorities had for some reason placed considerable importance on students showing up at the beginning of the semester.

---

7 Ajaccio is an uninteresting town and is therefore only superficially touched upon in this story. Like many other Mediterranean towns it has a beautiful and appealing façade and a dirty and scary back side, with narrow streets and an extraordinary quantity of excrement. The name Ajaccio, from what has been said, is derived from *Augias*, the name of the king whose stalls Heracles was set to clean. He did this by directing the Alpheus River through the shit, and you can still see the remnants of the big water pipes he built for the occasion. The improvements he brought were only temporary – the water pipes deteriorated and the unsanitary levels quickly regained their former level.

We agreed that the money we had left must be used for an SOS telegram to our rich friend Max in Zurich. He would have to become the supporter who rescued the expedition and brought it back to the starting point. But then we would have to count on spending at least one day in Nice, and how would we finance our stay? There are only two possibilities, George said: we can settle down on the beach, buy a little bread and wine and spend the night in our sleeping bags; or we can check into a hotel. The latter option was the best, because we would then have an address from which to send the telegram request to Max (we were already counting on it as a certainty). So – hotel.

It is true that the hotel receptionists on the Riviera have a sadly sceptical attitude where credit to bums is concerned, and we could not expect to be taken for anything else.

George had an idea. 'We have to go to the most expensive luxury hotel,' he said. 'Then there is a chance we'll be taken for eccentric American millionaires.'

I thought it was far more plausible that we would be taken for a cheap version of eccentric American comedians, but George stuck to his guns.

We finally agreed that George should make an attempt, albeit without his ice axe and rope. George chose the Hotel Ruhl et des Anglais, which was then the most expensive and snobbish hotel on the Riviera. Max and I stayed humbly in the background, both because we thought the sight of the three of us at once would be too unnerving for a normal head receptionist and also because with our familiarity with George we thought of the possibility that he might end up in a combative involvement with the doorman. Five minutes later George came out of the hotel in a fairly humbled state. He had been met with the most exquisitely cool politeness – they truly regretted, but the hotel was full.

So there we stood. We had the distinct impression that no matter which hotel we approached, it would be fully occupied. Then Carlo Bonelli came out through the revolving door and greeted us with overwhelming enthusiasm. He explained that he had come over the day before on his own boat and now lived at the Ruhl – the director was a relative – or maybe he was a business associate.

'You see, George,' I said when we later in the day were sitting at table with Uncle Carlo in his salon, 'once in a while it is good to have relatives.'

George could not deny that this sometimes provided practical advantages, but generally he was probably more interested in enemies.

When on the following day we bid farewell to Carlo at the railroad station, George had wrested a promise from him of an immediate invitation to the colony in the event developments down there should take a turn toward less peaceful circumstances. He never received such an invitation. This certainly was not related to any lack of hospitality or with the bandits not liking George, quite the opposite. One would have to look far (and in vain) to find more hospitable people than Corsican *banditos*, and George was certainly a youngster after their own heart.

It is a strange thing. Every once in a while you can end up in a situation that leads to a temporary shortage of one or more kinds of merchandise, and the result is, as you know, what we call rationing. There is reason to believe that we must have come to Corsica at a time when, probably because of excessive use, there was a suspicious lack of private enemies. This sad situation then made it necessary to reserve that merchandise for the Corsicans.

About the author

Alf Bonnevie Bryn (1889–1949) was a Norwegian mountaineer, author and engineer. Throwing himself into his passion for climbing while studying in Switzerland, he not only co-founded the Norsk Tindeklub mountaineering club but made several first ascents in 1910, including the Norwegian peaks of Stetind, Trakta and Klokketind. After graduating, Bryn went on to have successful careers as both an engineer and author, publishing a series of detective novels. His most popular work remains *Tinder og Banditter* – 'Peaks and Bandits', first published in 1943, which recounts his climbing escapades in Corsica with George Ingle Finch in 1909.